D1592492

Words
from the
SOURCE

Words
from the
SOURCE

Brad Steiger

PRENTICE-HALL, INC.
Englewood Cliffs, New Jersey

10 9 8 7 6 5 4 3

Library of Congress Cataloging in Publication Data

Steiger, Brad.
    Words from the source.

    Includes index.
    1. Psychical research.   2.   Occult sciences.
1. Title
BF1031.S7684   133.9   74-25571
ISBN 0-13-963348-0

Contents

Words
from the
SOURCE

1

Sharing the Things Worth Having

"Love is the strongest positive emotion and strength. It far outbalances that of hate."

"Work with the laws of the universe, and you will have everything. Work against them, and you will have nothing, because you have cut off the flow. Flow is important, vastly important."

"You do not seek happiness. You *become* happiness: And it becomes you."

"If you can't share something, it isn't worth having."

A man named Louis made each of the above statements, and he speaks often of love, of flowing with the universe, of finding meaningful happiness, and of sharing one's insights and joys with others. Louis lives in a rambling old inn on Orcas Island, one of the San Juan group, just off the coast of Washington state. The inn is named Outlook, and its name symbolizes the universal vision and the reaching-out of Louis and those friends of his who have gathered to work and teach for the Louis Foundation.

In the summer of 1972, my family and I traveled to Orcas

Island to spend a week with the Louis family. My daughters were soon delightedly helping to wait on tables in the dining room. My wife was matching her culinary skills with Jon's in the kitchen. My sons were doing their best to keep up with Starr Farish in his multiplicity of roles as Louis' administrative assistant, chief handyman, and business manager. Our family had soon merged with Louis' family—Helen Haberly, his ever-cheerful, super-efficient secretary; Effie, his cleaning lady with her Mrs. Santa Claus disposition; the young people who come to learn as students and serve as waiters, repairmen, and gardeners; the friends who regularly visit with their own stores of metaphysical knowledge and volunteer labor.

Gina Cerminara, a dear friend of Louis' and my much-respected colleague, first introduced me to Louis through a letter. It was Gina's suggestion that since I had written a number of biographies of talented psychic-sensitives, I should direct my efforts toward an examination of the life of Louis. Louis and I did meet in Hawaii, where we were both participants in a metaphysical conference; but I found him rather aloof to the idea of a biography. It was Louis' conviction that in his case, his work was of far more importance than a chronicle of his life. But he was receptive to the suggestion that I might select and edit a number of the teachings which he had received over the past several years through his channeling with the Source.

"I would like to see the book become an instrument of teaching, of metaphysical instruction," Louis said. "I think the public is growing weary with accounts of psychics solving crimes, chasing ghosts, and finding missing rings. Those things are exciting, and in some cases worthwhile, of course. But I believe the person who has been turned on to metaphysics is now searching for a direction, a way of going. I would like my book to be placed on one's nightstand, a book to be used as a steady source of both inspiration and reference."

It is to be hoped that Louis' thoughts and wishes have been realized in this present volume.

Although teaching and sharing are the main points of

emphases in the book, I did manage to convince Louis that readers would appreciate receiving information regarding certain vital statistics of his life:

Louis: I was born in the Southwest in the summer. My mother and father were just youngsters, around seventeen or eighteen, when I was born. They had been in love since they had been children.

My mother's mother had been a professional psychic, evidently very good, from all the reports we have. She was a very frail woman, and Mother has always believed that all the readings Grandmother gave sapped her strength and resulted in her early death. She had been trained as a nurse before she immigrated from Bergen, Norway; and she would give readings day or night for a quarter or fifty cents. So, naturally, from the very first inkling of my psychic abilities, my mother has always been very solicitious about my health.

You have said that Edgar Cayce gave your mother a pre-birth reading concerning you and your future life which has proved accurate.

Yes. I don't really know where my parents met Cayce or how they heard about him. I think it was probably in Texas, because he was going down there from time to time to search for oil deposits. Anyway, I have always been under the impression that they met in Texas. They evidently struck quite a rapport with Cayce, and there was a lot of correspondence back and forth.

So one time my mother was having coffee with Mr. Cayce, and he told her that she was with child. She didn't really understand the kind of biblical verbiage he so often employed, so she asked, "Do you mean I'm pregnant?" And Mr. Cayce answered: "I guess that is another way of putting it."

As I understand it, Mr. Cayce then volunteered to do a reading on my mother's unborn son. A lot of the reading had to do with my mother's past lives. He told her about a physical condition that would not develop for twenty years. It must have been present in embryonic form, for she went to the

Mayo Clinic to be operated on for the condition about twenty-five years after the reading.

Mr. Cayce told Mother that I had been a seer in China at the time of the Boxer Rebellion, and he said that I had badly perverted my clairvoyant gifts. He told her that in the present lifetime I would be a difficult child to raise. He was certainly correct on that score! I'm not proud to admit that once I learned that I was different from others, I often used my abilities to my advantage. My mother had a very difficult and uncomfortable time delivering me. I guess for a while the doctors feared they might lose my mother.

Well, anyway, Mr. Cayce went on to say that I would be able to do things similar to the things he could do. He said that I would be received by kings and queens—which I have—that I would write books and that books would be written about me; that I would be widely known as a seer.

Interestingly, the reading specified that one day I would dwell on Orcas Island and that here a "star" would come into my life. Through a most remarkable chain of circumstances I have come to live on Orcas Island, and perhaps equally strange is the manner in which I met Mr. J. Starr Farish and how he came to be very much in the picture in our work here on the island. You know, for the longest time I kept searching the skies each evening, looking for that "star" to manifest itself. It was only after Starr and I met at the home of a mutual friend that I realized this "star" would come from Seattle, not from space.

I was very thin, very frail as a child. One doctor told my mother that because of a heart condition, I would not live to be five years old. Then after I attained that age, he changed it to six years old. He kept upping the date of my death until I reached adulthood.

As far back as my mind goes, I remember seeing auras around people. I didn't always know what these colors were or what they represented, but I have always seen them. And, of course, I just assumed everyone else saw them as well.

I have never discussed this before, but when I was a child, there was a lovely man who used to appear to me occasionally—

especially if I were very troubled. He would come to me and talk to me. He was a great deal of help to me, because from the very beginning of my life, I felt very uncomfortable, very displaced, as if I were an alien who did not really belong here.

Although the people with whom I lived were kind to me and were very loving, they didn't talk right. They didn't smell right; they didn't dress right. I loved them, but I never really felt a part of them. It is interesting, but I never really felt at home anywhere until I was about nine years of age, when I went to the Orient with my grandmother.

Did you have a name for this man who came to see you when you were troubled?

He never gave me a name. Many times he would sit on my bed and talk to me for long periods of time. He had very long white hair and a beard; and he looked very "disciplish"—you know, what one thinks of as one of the disciples of Jesus. He wore a robe or tunic.

I know the psychologists will think they have a clue to the inner workings of my mind when they read this. "Aha," they will say, "the lad had a problem, so he fantasized a teacher, a mentor to give him courage."

Did the man have an Oriental appearance?

No, he was not an Oriental. He would tell me of things that were coming up in my life and how I could handle them. I was always wide-awake when he appeared. It wasn't a dream thing.

He had such good vibes. The first time that I ever saw him, when I was just a very small boy, I looked into those nice big eyes so filled with love and compassion, and I just knew that he was a good man. It got so I could even feel his hand when he would pat me on my head.

As I became older, his visits became longer. He was a great solace to me, because my family didn't quite know how to cope with me. My friends didn't know what I was. But he made me feel good and clean and sane and not alone.

Did anyone else ever see him?

No, in fact I have never spoken about him to anyone, because I have always felt his visits were a kind of sacred thing. And I was never certain anyone would understand me. When I was a boy, you know, a lot of people laughed at me in a very cruel way.

Did they stop laughing when your predictions began coming true?

Yes, but then the laughter was often replaced by something akin to worship, and that was just as bad.

When I was about nine years old, I used my clairvoyance to locate a boy who had been missing in the mountains outside of Phoenix. The story leaked out and made the wire services. There were all sorts of human interest stories about the "boy with the X-ray eyes."

One day we opened our curtains to find our yard filled with people. Ripley wanted me to tour with his "Believe It or Not" freak show. A cult in the area had been waiting for a promised boy messiah, and they decided that I must be the holy child. Our poor lawn was literally trampled brown.

How did your peer group react? Did they begin to revere you as well?

They would look at me sort of funny, you know, then they would sing funny little rhymes. They had all sorts of names for me.

And my teachers would take me back to the cloakrooms and ask for readings! "Is John going to marry me?" "Shall I buy a new car now or wait until fall?" Even the principal called me into her office on some pretext and asked me for a reading once we were alone.

What kind of student were you?

Not a very good one. I was always sitting looking out the window and dreaming. I read a great deal, though, but applied little of that knowledge to my classes.

About this time I started gaining weight, so I began doing a lot of art work rather than playing athletics. I would cry easily; and, of course, boys of ten and eleven just weren't supposed to cry. I had a lot of fights, and usually the boys would beat me up, because I just wasn't any good at fighting.

But then at night my friend would appear and explain to me that I should not feel so rejected. He said that the other people just did not understand about certain things that really mattered. He would calm me so that I could go to sleep. With his encouragement, I began to do more and more readings and my family came to accept me more and more.

I haven't seen him since I was a boy, so I guess it hasn't been necessary for him to come to talk with me.

Did he say good-bye the last time you saw him?

Yes, he told me that I would not be needing him any more. He told me that I had come to work with people. He said that my needs would always be taken care of, but not always my wants. He repeated this a number of times.

Starr Farish's aunt, Betty Otis, is, to the best of her knowledge, the first person outside of Edgar Cayce's immediate family circle to have benefited from the healing talents of the famous "sleeping prophet." She was kind enough to talk with me and to provide me with a description of the comparisons between Louis and Edgar Cayce working in the trance state:

> This was in 1911. My uncle, Frank Mohr, owned some mines in Hopkinsville, Kentucky, where Edgar Cayce lived. He had heard of this man and how he could help his family by going to sleep. I had suffered infantile paralysis, and I could only drag my crippled leg. The doctors termed me a hopeless case, and said that I should be prepared to be a cripple for the rest of my life.
>
> Thank goodness my family didn't accept this diagnosis. Since they were in an agitated and confused state over me, Uncle Frank asked Mr. Cayce if he could help us. Edgar Cayce agreed to Uncle Frank's request, and my uncle brought his own secretary along to take notes on the reading. I still have this original reading.
>
> My parents followed to the letter the treatment Mr. Cayce recommended. It was a matter of massage with cocoa butter for two hours every day for two years. It worked. I have lived a perfectly normal life, and very few people can detect that I had any lameness at all. I should mention that Elizabeth Wilson was my maiden name. There are several readings in the Cayce files which bear my name.
>
> Through the years my family would always go to Mr. Cayce with any kind of serious problem. Uncle Frank was cured of blindness through some kind of poultices recommended by Mr. Cayce. My

father had a serious illness in 1924, and Mr. Cayce's reading told us to go to a certain river and get buckets of mud for packs. We had to be pretty underhanded about this. Not only did we not dare tell the doctor what we were doing, but we had to keep it quiet from our friends as well. But my dad got well after the doctors had given up.

How would I compare what I experienced as an observer of Mr. Cayce with what I am now experiencing as an observer of Louis? I would like to say that the two men have this in common: They are both quiet, peace-loving souls.

I remember sitting beside Mr. Cayce in the front-porch swing one afternoon after he had finished a reading for my grandmother. Uncle Frank had come to get me, because he wanted me to see Mr. Cayce give a reading. He said it was something I should remember all of my life. So we sat on the porch afterward, and I recall sitting by Mr. Cayce. He was just quiet, loving, and he seemed to have a dreamy kind of feeling. He didn't talk about anything metaphysical or anything over my head. He used common, ordinary conversation, just as Louis does today when he sits down and talks with us.

Both Mr. Cayce and Louis lie prone when giving readings. I keep talking about Mr. Cayce as though he were here today, but that is the way I felt about it when I was observing Louis this morning in deep trance. I had the feeling that I was once again a girl of ten observing Mr. Cayce in trance—only this time it is my nephew Starr in control instead of my Uncle Frank!

I have seen other psychics and mediums in trance, but they were either sitting or standing, and they seemed to be half-awake. Neither Mr. Cayce nor Louis seem half-awake. In fact, they seem more dead than alive to me. It seems as though there is a corpse lying there with that very soft voice coming out of it.

Louis, I noticed, is covered by a blanket; Mr. Cayce was not. Mr. Cayce lay with his hands over his solar plexus, whereas Louis' hands are down at his sides.

I have not had any personal experience of healing by Louis, as I had with Mr. Cayce; but I have not asked for any. I have, though, had two people very close to me who have had healing experiences with Louis. In each case, Louis presented them with an immediate diagnosis and prescribed a regimen of diet, exercise, and vitamins to follow. In each case, there was a prompt and effective healing.

One thing which occurs to me in discussing my experiences with these two men is not so much the differences in the men as the differences in the times. In the time of Mr. Cayce, everything was sub rosa—hush-hush. You would hardly dare to tell your best friends about him. There was no question but that you would be scoffed at, and Mr. Cayce might have been in danger if the authorities had learned of his healing work. Now things are much more open. If Louis were to prescribe something for me, with the kind of doctor I have, I would go right to him and tell him about Louis' recommendation. My doctor would welcome some extra help. I am sure that all doctors are not as open-minded as mine, but times have changed. I have often wondered if there is a cosmic or karmic reason for our family's being connected with these two similar and very unique men. Perhaps one day we will find out.

When my family and I visited Louis at the Outlook Inn in June of 1972, I was permitted to enter the master bedroom which serves as his *sanctum sanctorum.* I sat on the foot of a king-sized bed which faced Louis lying blanketed on a sofa before a crackling fireplace. Starr Farish adjusted the quilt about the mystic's chest and placed a hand on his shoulder, as Louis began the deep breathing that seemed to help bring about the trance state.

The fireplace mantel supported a large mirror, a cross with "Love" stamped across its center, three candles in a linked holder, and a variety of incense burners. A string of temple bells hung at the side of the fireplace. The door to Starr's study was just to the right.

To my left were three shelves heavily covered with potted plants. A large Buddha smiled serenely down at me from the top shelf. To my right was a portrait of Gautama Buddha, a painting of American Indian corn maidens, and a number of walking sticks. A dresser top bore a large bust of Jesus and the familiar statuary of Dürer's praying hands. Three shelves of books served as an intellectual backdrop for the spiritual artifacts.

Behind the entranced Louis were another dresser, literally entwined with flowering plants; a framed copy of the *Desiderata;* the well-known painting of the Last Supper; a closeup portrait of Jesus at the Lord's Table; a map of the heavens;

and a writing table with a study lamp. The table also bore a tape recorder, and Starr held its tiny microphone scant inches from Louis' mouth as the soft-whisper voice representative of the Source channeled its messages through the entranced mystic.

Jean Mayo was working for Aquarius Electronics when she first met Louis. The electronics firm had developed an analyzer capable of measuring the brain waves of an individual and feeding them back to him so that he might train his brain to enter various levels of activity for learning or meditative activities. Jean had worked with Dr. Stanley Krippner at the Maimonides Hospital Dream Laboratory and had assisted with the experiments which sought to influence the dream state through telepathic transfer of images.

Early in 1972, Jean met Dr. Irene Hickman, who invited Jean to accompany her to an international conference on psychic healing being conducted in Honolulu. Dr. Hickman was to give a lecture on alpha rhythms, and she asked Jean to help her demonstrate the power of mind energy in turning light projectors on and off. Dr. Hickman also offered Jean the opportunity to measure the brain waves of a number of internationally famous healers and psychics.

Jean Mayo: I had begun to notice a pattern when a psychic was doing a reading or a healing which repeated a beta-theta 60/40 percent flicker response. Sometimes the psychic would close his eyes and go into 40 percent alpha, then come back into the beta-theta with no alpha in between. Since I saw this pattern being repeated, and it was a pattern that I had not seen on other people, I was beginning to think that there was, perhaps, a pattern to a certain kind of psychic activity. I was becoming quite excited about it when I met Louis.

Louis was willing to have me hook up his head while he did his thing, though at that time, I didn't know what Louis' thing was. He wanted to lie down on the bed, and because the reading I was getting was so different from some of the other psychics I had measured, I thought that he might be lying on the electrode, thereby preventing us from getting an accurate reading. I kept checking all of my plugs to be certain that they were actually recording Louis' brain waves.

About that time, this deep whispered voice, for which I was totally unprepared, said, "You cannot measure God. You are measuring Louis' physiological reactions only. He is to be comprehended, not measured."

I wasn't sure what else to expect, but the voice went on to give several helpful readings, one to Dr. Irene, and one to myself. The voice prescribed a diet on which I subsequently lost thirty pounds, so I was very happy to have received that reading.

I asked if I would give up my work, and the answer was no. The brain wave analyzer was a fascinating toy, the voice said. It would teach people that they are more than a body, that they have a mind, too—a mind that may be brought under control, but which is incapable of being measured.

Louis' brain waves were quite different from most people's brain waves. In his trance state he was not specifically beta-theta. He was not an alpha person, nor was he in the high amplitude energy output. As a matter of fact, in his trance state, he was in such a low energy field that his brain waves produced a noise which on our machine indicates a very low amplitude. He was in beta-alpha-theta, continuously flickering all over the dial at a very low amplitude, none of it above twenty microamps. It was as though he had actually set his physiology aside so that this other voice could speak through him.

There were so many questions bubbling through my brain that I knew that I must have another session. I asked Tim Scully of Aquarius Electronics to fly us up to Orcas Island, so that we might wire Louis for some more tests. Louis was really sweet about it. He was happy to have us come.

For the second reading, he again went into a trance. Apparently the body gets cold, because Starr always wraps Louis in a blanket and builds a fire, even though it may be a warm day.

Again, the wave pattern dropped down into a low amplitude and into a variety all over the dial, which means up into the noise range very fast, very low amplitude, down into the alphas and to the thetas. I didn't notice any deltas. There were quite a few betas, of course; but there was no holding pattern of any kind that I could discern.

I asked the Source whether the training of alpha waves was good for people, and the voice said yes. The procedure could teach people how to relax.

I asked what we were really measuring, and this whispery voice said that we were accurately measuring but a very small portion of what was actually going on; and that as it said before, there was a lot going on in the brain that could not be measured, that we were getting physiological reactions to certain processes.

I asked about theta training, and it said that such training would be very helpful for people such as scientists, who lived in the concrete world, who dealt exclusively with facts and figures. Theta training, the voice went on, could give such men and women insight into the other creative working levels of the brain.

For those people who lived primarily in the creative and abstract realms, the voice said that they should take off their shoes and wander through a field of clover. Man, it commented, is a dynamic structure, and he must relate to other dynamic structures, such as trees, mountains, and streams. In such places, a renewal of the spirit takes place which cannot happen in a concrete jungle.

It has been a beautiful experience for me to meet such a loving person as Louis. Since I met him, I have been through a number of transition periods, and right in the middle of a very heavy one, I received a wonderful letter from Louis without having informed him of my difficulties. He told me that I was going through a very heavy transition period, but that I should remember the central purpose of my life and stay tuned in, rather than getting caught up in the outer manifestations.

It was very reassuring to know that Louis was not only tuned in to me in the middle of all that confusion, but that he was loving and caring. I am very grateful that I met Louis and

12

that he has been willing to share some of his visions and insights with me.

Jean Mayo has now become one of thousands who have learned through direct contact with the loving, caring Louis just precisely what the mystic means when he says, "If you can't share a thing, it isn't worth having."

2

A Dialogue
with the Source

At 7:45 A.M. on Sunday, February 22, 1970, Starr Farish sought to engage the Source of Louis' channeled material in a dialogue that would more clearly delineate and define its identity.

Starr Farish: You have told me a couple of times that you were always with me. You have said, "How can you be so blind?" Well, I don't mean to be so blind, but I don't understand what you mean when you say such things.

There once was a man who went about the world proclaiming how empty of funds he was, and yet, in his pocket, there was a bar of gold.

But you are talking about two different things, aren't you? One is materialistic and the other is spiritual reality.

They are actually the same thing, only they are at two different levels of vibration. One is lower, and one is at a more rapid pace. You see, you must learn to transcend—transcend and transmute.

Every situation—and we emphasize *every* situation—has many levels of consciousness to it. If you will start perceiving things on many levels of consciousness, then and only then can you start working with Universal Principles. You get so caught up in your interpretation of things [that] you do not stop to think that there may be other points of view.

Or the point of view?

Yes. Last night we heard you proclaiming what you seemed to believe were hard and fast rules to your life. You know, there are no hard, set rules to anything. So stop saying that it must be this way, or it must be that way—just start *knowing*. Start *expecting*. Start *anticipating*.

You cannot separate your life and segment it by saying, "This is my spiritual life, this is my other life." You have but one life, you know, and you must live the whole of your life under one rule. You must cease being two people. You must become one individual. Start being yourself. From today on, let us go forward.

But I get so enmeshed in things.

If you think you do, you do. Remember, as a man thinketh, so he is.

If a man has problems, if he has insecurities, it started with his thinking processes. That is a fact. That is a principle, and neither you nor anyone else can side-step.

As you change your thinking pattern, you change the rest of the pattern. It is really very simple, almost as if you were driving an automobile. If you want to turn left, you simply turn the wheel to the left. You're surely strong enough to do this.

Yes, I can do that.

You have been wondering with whom you are talking. Would it surprise you if we told you that you are talking with no one?

No person?

That is true. To equate it to your terms, you are communicating with a force field, a collection of energy that is being housed for the moment in Louis' body. You are seeing his lips move, and you are seeing his body, yet it is not *his* energy that is causing his lips to move. This is why he does not get tired. He suffers no energy loss. It is as if he were sleeping.

16

You are a collection of energies, then, which are housed in Louis' body for awhile.

Yes, an intelligence, an awareness. That's simple, isn't it?

Did Edgar Cayce also house such a collection of energies?

Yes.

Are you what Louis means when he speaks of "the boys upstairs"?

That makes it easier for Louis to comprehend. Louis is a very romantic person, and this analogy makes him feel comfortable.

But energy is everywhere, isn't it? So you are, in essence, everywhere.

Yes, only we represent a collective energy, a unified energy force field. You see, ordinarily energy flows like a stream or a river. But in this instance, this energy is housed in a body. It is collected together in a molecular structure. But it does not flow as it ordinarily would, because it is gathered together for a specific purpose.

We tell you these things because you are filled with so many questions. We're trying to make you happy.

Why was Louis so disturbed yesterday?

He allows the mutterings of the individuals about him to disturb him. It would be well if you would act as a buffer in such situations. People are supposed to come to this place to learn and to grow, not be concerned with all the little if's, and's, and but's.

It does not matter if Louis parts his hair on the right side or the left side, and this is not something that others should concern themselves with. People should heed the message, not the messenger. Would you please pass this along to others.

Tell them also that they are here to expand, not to bicker. Such conversation is destructive.

We need at this place a very loving vortex. Every time dissension occurs, it destroys joy, harmony, tranquility, and peace. Tell these people that if they cannot abide in harmony, they *must* go. We have proclaimed this place to be a place of God, where Divine Harmony is to rule.

Be very direct, very firm.

All right, let us proceed.

Can I have more instructional dreams, like the one I recently had?

Your other consciousness asked for this dream as a way of bringing this information into your reality consciousness. Relax, and you can bring more things to you. Relax and let go. Pretend that you are a pot of soup bubbling. See yourself warm, without form, flowing.

You too, have a mission, and it must come before all things.

Louis is going to Phoenix to see about his income tax. It's not necessary that I go there, is it?

That's not a mission, is it? Is he being *called* to do his income tax? We speak of missions, not of all these other frivolities and trivialities. But if he is called on a mission, your place is right beside him.

Now let us talk about the forthcoming trip a bit. As usual, there will be many who will be trying to get to Louis. Some will say, "Love, love." Some will say, "Interest, interest." Some will say that they are going to help. But it will behoove you to see through the insincere. Treat them kindly, but do not let them sap Louis' strength.

This trip can be most important in that you can establish a Light Center in this city. You see, the whole idea is to establish spiritual centers throughout the land.

Let us explain the Louis Foundation to you a bit more. In your terms, let us say that the Louis Foundation is like a dynamo; and from this large vortex, or dynamo, will run wires to various other places. The Louis Foundation will supply the energy by which these other Light Centers will function. Do you see the picture?

Yes, but the Light Centers in the other cities do not have to be physical, do they? I mean, like a hall or something.

There needs to be a gathering together of people, yes. Remember the Master Jesus said, "Where two or more are gathered together in my name, I shall be there also." Now, he was not speaking of his physical body, but of his light, his energy, his force field. You see, this can all be reduced down to magnetic principles, to electronic principles. When people gather together at these Light Centers, it charges their spiritual batteries. That is the whole idea. When these people charge their batteries, they will cause their auras, their vibrational force fields, to expand; and they will go about and touch other peoples' lives, which in turn will charge their batteries.

How may I speak with you when Louis isn't around?

You cannot. We need his body in order to function through him.

Are you something like intuition?

We can impress things upon your mind, yes. We can communicate with you, but not on a verbal level. Somehow you like to hear the words. When we speak directly to you through Louis, the words seem to have more meaning for you. This is well and good.

May we speak of meditation?

When one meditates, he is actually unifying himself with reality.

With you?

With reality. We are only a part of that reality. Call that reality God, call it Universal Consciousness—it has many labels.

When one meditates, he is cognizant on many levels of the One-ment that unifies. This is the whole reason for meditation. How you go about meditation does not really matter. You can stand on your head and meditate. You can run around the block and meditate. You can swim and meditate. Meditation is a moment of realization. It does not really matter how that moment comes about.

Various people are influenced by various methods. Usually it is acceptable to relax the physical body, to free the mental faculties. Every time that one is meditating, he is walking up a ladder of awareness. This is a step-by-step process.

In one of his lessons, Louis said meditation was concentration, contemplation, and release. I didn't know what he meant by release.

Release means letting go of the mental processes. It means letting go of "Should I get some gasoline?" "Should I scratch my nose?" "How am I going to pay this bill?" You see, if you have a bird and you release it, it flies away. Once you release yourself from all these trivialities, you will start to fly and soar. This is how one raises his consciousness.

But remember, you cannot unify with the Real and remain imbued with the Artificial. You must choose between the two. You cannot turn right and left at the same time.

Why do I get a chance to live?

Existing is the artificial, the false. Millions and millions of people are caught up in this pattern. Few people live.

You are beginning to live because you deserve it. We give no gifts. We do not barter. Forget your "how come's" and your "what if's" and remember one word: *Be.*

Now, to bring up another matter, Louis has said that he shouldn't give readings on a full stomach.

He can do readings regardless of the condition of his stomach, but for the welfare of his physical vehicle . . . Well, let us explain to you what takes place when Louis does these readings.

For the moment, his body is dead. He is dead. Consequently, there is no digestion going on. If food has been recently placed in the body, it lies there and cannot be digested. It lies there and putrifies.

Have you noticed when Louis awakens from a session that he is always very hungry? He is like a newborn babe, and a newborn babe always wants food. He is really not hungry, but it is merely a reaction to the session. That is also why Louis gets so cold. His circulation stops. Everything stops. If you were to place a stethoscope on his heart, you would find that it is barely beating.

When you enter his body, do you sometimes have more energy than at other times?

Yes, depending on the situation.

You seem to have good energy this morning.

Yes, we usually know the situation in advance.

What is time to you?

Time is but a word. It is one of your playtoys. We don't need playtoys. We *are.*

3

God, Manifested and Unmanifested

A woman once asked Louis what he meant when he spoke of God. Louis responded by saying that there was nothing that he could conceive of that is not God, either manifested or unmanifested. "We carry God around within us," he commented. "Everything that we look and see and touch is a part of this thing called God. Everything is part of the one whole."

Would it be correct to say, God is man and man is God?
That is one way of saying it. God is all things. We cannot limit it to man. God is the flower, the tree. God flows through all things, all manifestation. Man should be expressing God, but many forget where they came from and of what they are a part.

How may I become more spiritually aware and learn to distinguish between spiritual and physical awareness?
There is basically one awareness, and it manifests itself in many forms with many ramifications. However, in essence, there is but one awareness, one God, one consciousness. One

cannot differentiate between physical awareness and spiritual awareness, for they are one and the same. One is in the realm of the manifested, and the other is in the realm of the unmanifested. They are the two sides of the coin.

As you become more aware of the unmanifested aspects of your totality, the other aspects of your totality also will reach a more aware state. As you balance your totality, everything about you will grow. It is all spirit. We cannot separate this thing called life and say, "These things are spiritual and these things are not." Everything is of the spirit; everything is of God. When we realize this on all levels, when our actions are in accordance with this principle, then we start making progress. It is important to know that your spiritual world is your *real* world and that your physical world is a reflection of the unmanifested world.

What is meant by the Father?

The Father is a principle. People confuse *the* Father with a physical father. The Father Principle is the unmanifested aspect of God. The Mother Principle is the manifested aspect of mankind. The earth, as man knows it, is Mother. The Father spirit uses the Earth-Mother as a vehicle. It is unfortunate that the earthplane, physical father becomes mixed-up with the non-Earth Father.

If we have the Father and Mother principles—I suppose one might say positive and negative polarities—as unmanifested and manifested, where does the Holy Ghost come in?

The Holy Ghost is a man-made concept. If man wanted to be accurate, he would say, the Father-Mother God.

I went to a wedding where the minister spoke of the Father who is most merciful. I tried to understand this.

The Father is neither merciful nor unmerciful. Mercy is a quality that human beings have.

The Father just is?

Yes. The Father is unmanifested love. The Mother is manifested love. Within the two principles of the One, there are polarities. Within the Mother Principle, there are negative and positive manifested. Within the Father Principle, there are negative and positive unmanifested.

22

Basically, on the Earth plane, we are concerned with the Mother Principle.

Yes, because the Earth plane is constantly procreating. Man plants seeds, and they come up, and they die, and there is this cycling that is constantly on-going. The Father Principle is a constant reservoir.

You [the Source] are of the Father Principle, aren't you?

Yes. Let us give you an image. The Mother Principle would be water going over a waterwheel. It goes over, goes down, and returns. Over, down, and returns. The Father Principle, in the water image, would be a lake.

But it takes the two principles to be a whole.

Yes. But one should avoid labels of any kind.

When men talk of their Father in heaven, they are really speaking of the spirit within each man. Man's spirit, his reservoir, is within him.

Remember that the basic underlying function of the Mother Principle is change. A stone will not remain a stone forever. One day it will break up, and in another day it will become soil. The soil will break down into minerals and sustain the plant kingdom. The sustenance of the plant will one day be the food for man or animals. All things on the Earth plane are part of such a cycle.

The Father Principle is the reservoir that allows this change to take place. It provides the energy, the essence to keep the cycles progressing.

Then where does the eternal and the non-eternal come in? It sounds as though the Mother Principle would be non-eternal, the way we're talking, because it is manifested. But it is really eternal because it is constantly changing. Is that correct?

It is eternal in the sense of manifested eternal. . . .

Because it may change shape or form.

Yes.

This chair may rot, but it is still eternal, because it is changing into something else.

Yes, but it still boils down to manifested and unmanifested.

Now do I understand? We have the totality, and we break that down into Father-Mother, but each Father-Mother breaks

23

down into its own positive and negative. If we go one step further, we find that each positive and negative of that sub-section has a positive and a negative of its own . . . and it just keeps breaking down.

Exactly.

Could one use the Chinese yin-yang symbol to represent this concept?

Yes, that is a very ancient symbol of God.

4

A Strange and Beautiful Man Named Leon

Louis knew him only as Leon, an enigmatic man of the Arizona desert with whom he lived for over two years. Leon, a man of great awareness, had come into this lifetime for the purpose of working with twelve students. Louis was one of those twelve, he was told, but he never learned by what manner of selection Leon had chosen him.

"There is the old adage that states that when the student is ready the teacher will appear," Louis reminded Starr, my wife, Marilyn, and myself, as he settled back in his favorite chair, warming to the subject of Leon, his master. "I had been crying out into space, 'I am ready!' And I had been growing increasingly frustrated by the silence that absorbed my plea."

One night in 1948, when Louis was living in California, he spotted a small newspaper ad which promoted an evening lecture by a rather well-known Spiritualist medium.

"I had heard the woman speak before and she was uninspiring in her presentation. She was a stout woman who had a large bust, wore pince-nez glasses, and smelled of talcum powder. Her lecture was filled with 'Oh, beloved ones,' 'Dear sons and daughters of light,' and that sort of metaphysical sugar talk.''

Louis started to fold the newspaper when something within him dictated that he must go to the woman's lecture that evening.

"There was quite a civil war going on inside of me, because one part of me definitely did not want to attend that lecture. The taxi fare alone would be three dollars and fifty cents, and that in itself was a lot to spend for nothing. But in the end I arrived in front of the lecture hall by bus.''

Soon Louis was seated on a hard wooden chair, and before he had time to reconsider his decision, the lecturer had appeared with her greetings from the spirit world to her "dearly beloved sons and daughters of light.''

"I had sat there about fifteen minutes," Louis recalled, "when a woman six rows down turned around and gave me a big smile. I thought, well, I don't remember reading for you, but I probably should since you are smiling so big. I gave her a return smile and tried to direct my attention back to the lecturer on the platform, who was really going strong at this point. This business of the woman turning around smiling at me went on five or six times during the evening, and all the time I was trying to remember who she was.

"After the lecture and the benediction, I just sort of sat there. Pretty soon this smiling woman approached me.

" 'You are Louis?' " she asked.

"I acknowledged that I was. 'I'm Jane Caldwell,' she went on. 'You have never met me, but I must talk to you.'

"I asked her if she had a car, and when she replied that she did, I suggested that she drive me back to my place where I could fix us some coffee and we could talk in private.''

Once in Louis' apartment, Jane Caldwell came directly to her purpose for having sought the sensitive's attention. "What I am going to tell you might seem rather strange," she said, "But I was told to take you somewhere. There is a man waiting for you who will be your teacher.''

Louis had had any number of strangers approach him with unusual requests and rather bizarre statements, but there was something about the woman and the manner in which she spoke which seemed to ring true.

"As she talked," Louis told us, "I could not help thinking that this woman knows whereof she speaks."

"When will you be ready to leave?" Jane Caldwell asked Louis.

He remembers telling her that he had a number of activities lined up in the immediate future, but somehow he heard himself telling her that he would be ready to leave in two days.

"We left San Bernardino in her car and continued to drive until we were in the Arizona desert near a small town named Morristown, which is located between Wickenburg and Phoenix. We arrived at our destination about three o'clock in the morning. After we had managed to travel this horrible dirt road full of chuckholes and dust, we finally came to a little shack. Its lights were on and there was a man standing in the door. He was a beautiful human being. He was Leon.

"I didn't know his age when I first met him. Certain people have told me various ages which he might have been. Someone said that Leon was ninety years old at the time we met. I don't know, I never saw a birth certificate. Strangely enough, although he had a long white beard and long white hair held back by a rubber band, he had a beautiful body, like that of a young boy's. He had no wrinkles in his face, and he had an extremely youthful bearing.

"He told me that he had been expecting me. He gave me a bit to eat, then ushered me to my bedroom—a little straw mat on the floor. I had been accustomed to a rather easy life of considerable comfort. Now my bed for the next two years would be nothing more than a little mat on the floor.

"My mind was reeling. Should I be here? Should I insist the woman take me back to San Bernardino? Then Leon stood beside me, placed his hand on me, and I dropped off to sleep."

The next morning, Jane Caldwell returned to California, and Louis remained with Leon.

"We were up at sunrise. For the next two years, our work would always begin at sunrise," Louis said. "There was always a teaching going on. The Tarot, the Cabala, the mystery schools—all sorts of studies.

"That first morning I went to the outhouse toilet and found a rattlesnake coiled up on a gunny sack. Since my early youth I had been taught that a coiled rattlesnake is an extremely dangerous creature. I let out a scream, and Leon came out of the house.

"Leon picked up the snake as you might pick up a garden hose, and he started talking to it. 'Berkely,' he said, 'Louis doesn't know that you haven't been feeling well and that I put you in here out of the elements. He has to use the outhouse. I'll put you back in after he is finished.' The snake just lay limply across his arms. It didn't even hiss. I often saw Leon pick up rattlesnakes in this manner."

Leon appeared to be of mixed parentage, perhaps East Indian and American. He made occasional mention of his father having been a sailor, and he spoke now and then of having spent some part of his life in New York City. But most of his life had been spent on the desert.

"We lived on this acreage of sand and rock, yet I spent some of the happiest days of my life on that seemingly barren land," Louis remarked. "Leon was a very exciting man. I never heard him say a negative statement. He never once got unhappy with me. And I asked some very stupid questions. Sometimes I would notice that he would become a bit tired of my ignorance and my endless questions. That was when he would say, 'Well, I think I am going to take a little walk out in the desert.' I suppose what he meant was that he would take a little walk so that he might get me out of his hair for a while.

"The man never sat idle. When we were not studying together, working together, he was chiseling big stones from the desert to fit the walls of the room he was adding to his house.

"Even though every day was very much like another, I suddenly realized that it would soon be Christmas. I am a great lover of the Christmas season. I know that Christmas is really in one's heart, that Christmas is really a spirit. I know all these things, but I also like the trappings. I really do love Christmas trees and decorations. Now here I was in this little shack out in the desert. There were no Christmas carols, no Christmas trees, no nothing. I was beginning to feel awfully strange inside.

"Of course, Leon sensed something was troubling me, so I told him the anxiety that I was experiencing with the passing of an unacclaimed Christmas. I said, 'Let's sit down and make each other a card or something.'

"Leon smiled and we went out in the desert and got a little paloverde tree. We took it home and placed it in some sand in an old lard can. We spent a whole day making ornaments out of tin cans. Leon did have a radio, and he tuned in a station that played Christmas carols.

"That night when I went to bed on my little mat, I looked over at the tree. The moonlight had come in and I swear that the tree was glowing as if it were in some Walt Disney story. When I awakened on Christmas morning, the whole tree was full of beautiful blossoms.

"Leon came in with a smile on his face and said, 'There is your Christmas present.' That was one of the nicest Christmases that I have ever had."

In spite of the lack of water and the dry dust of the area, Louis remembers that Leon insisted upon being always personally clean. "I learned to take baths with a cup of water," Louis laughed. "I would take a little washcloth, soak it with water, get it soapy, then rub all over. Then I would take that cup and carefully rinse myself."

Dietary indulgences were extremely frugal and sparse. "When Leon said, 'Let's have a cup of coffee,' that is what he meant—a cup. Breakfast was a cup of coffee and a piece of bread. Later in the day, maybe around two o'clock, we would have another piece of bread and some cheese. Sometimes before we would turn in at night, we would have another cup of coffee. That was the food for the day. Occasionally, though, I would go into town—and Leon did like mint ice cream. I would get some and bring it out to the desert and we would eat ice cream."

Louis is still impressed by the attitude which Leon expressed toward the living creatures of the desert with which he shared his domain. "Leon had a St. Francis attitude toward

29

the animals," Louis stated. He would always carry little crumbs and goodies for the birds and the rabbits. They would come to him and receive food from his hands. There was a communication between Leon and the animals. He had them all named. Every day they would come around the back step of the house and he would talk to them and pet them.

"Leon had about six hundred and forty acres, and he had decreed that all creatures would live together in peace and harmony while they were on his land. Ordinarily, the coyote eats the rabbit for his food, but on Leon's land, you would see them trotting side by side. Perhaps as soon as they left Leon's property, the coyote might pounce upon the rabbit, but as long as any creature was on Leon's territory, nothing ever fought or tried to destroy another living thing."

Brad Steiger: Who had Leon's teacher been?
Louis: No one that I knew of. He frequently made statements that he had studied with such-and-such a person, but I don't know if he actually was taught as he taught me. He was a very wise man.
Steiger: Did you ever find out when and why and how you were selected to be one of the twelve students?
Louis: No. And I was always afraid to ask in case there might have been a mistake made! You know, at first I didn't really feel as though I belonged there. I didn't really feel qualified. Some people have said that Leon was a master. I know that he was a very aware man, an illuminated man, a very loving person, very gentle, very wise.
Starr Farish: Tell them about the people who would try to take pictures of Leon.
Louis: Occasionally people would stop by and attempt to take pictures of Leon; I suppose because they thought him a colorful old desert rat. Most of the time there would just be a blur where Leon stood. I would ask him why it was that people couldn't take his picture, and he would smile and say, "Oh, you know, those cameras are defective." I don't know just exactly what did take place.
Farish: But he let your brother take a picture of him.

Louis: Yes. My brother came one time and took a picture of Leon, and it was all right.

Farish: Did you tell Brad and Marilyn how Leon got his money?

Louis: Now, Starr, so many things sound awfully weird when one just tells about them.

Steiger: How did he get his money? You can't leave us hanging.

Louis: He would go out far away beyond the rim of the mountains, and when he came back he would have a little bag full of gold. He said he knew where the gold was growing, and he would go periodically to "harvest" it.

Once I spoke to the assay man about Leon's gold, and he said that the strange thing about it was that it had characteristics of gold from areas far away from Arizona. I guess gold has peculiar characteristics which makes it possible for assayers to identify the region from which it has been taken. Montana gold, for instance, would be different from Arizona or New Mexico gold.

I tried to question Leon as to just exactly where he obtained his gold, but he would never volunteer any information about it, so I let it go. He would take his little bag to town and there would be just enough money to buy the supplies that we needed.

Marilyn Steiger: What about this woman who drove you to Leon's home. Did you ever learn more about her?

Louis: The woman was his wife, but she was not a wife as you would ordinarily think of a wife. She had been a disciple or whatever. I don't think they were ever formally married. I don't think they ever slept together as man and wife. She sort of looked after him and cleaned and things.

Steiger: Once a week or something like that?

Louis: Oh, no, she lived there most of the time. She had her own little place to sleep. Leon was considerably older than she was.

Marilyn: And she was also his disciple?

Louis: Not in the strict definition of the term. She had great respect for Leon. I heard later that she had come to him when she was extremely ill. Leon had made her well and saved her life. She decided to stay on and take care of him, since he was all alone out in the desert.

Farish: How many hours a day did you say Leon meditated?

Louis: He used to meditate three or four hours every day.

Steiger: Did Leon ever indicate who the other eleven students were?

Louis: No. I asked him about that one time and he said that I would know one day. To this day, I don't know, however.

Marilyn: How did you learn that Leon had passed on?

Farish: I had written to the lady about a question that I didn't want to bother Louis with. When she replied, she told me that Leon left the body on April 10, 1971.

Louis: When I touched the letter, I felt what it would tell me, but I didn't want to admit it. We aren't supposed to weep about such things, but we do, you know. Starr opened the letter and got a terrible look on his face. Later I found him weeping in the chapel, and I knew for certain that the letter had told of Leon's passing.

Marilyn: Starr, did you ever meet Leon?

Farish: No, but he knew about me. Just prior to his death, he sent me a stone via Louis. Louis put it in my hand as we were driving up the freeway from the airport. The stone has such magnificent vibrations that I got all teary-eyed. I guess it was a very receptive time on my part to receive the stone.

Louis: I had gone for a brief visit with Leon. We were walking in the desert, as was our custom, and every once in a while he would stop the lesson and point out something of nature to discuss. I told Leon that I must soon begin to think of catching my plane back to Seattle. We were walking through what in Arizona we call a "wash," a depression through which water will run when there is rain, and he reached down in the soil and picked up this rock. "Take this to Starr," he said. I put it in the pocket of my corduroy jacket and told him I would deliver it.

Then Leon told me that we would not be seeing one another again. "But if you ever really need me," he said, "I will be there to help you."

I know that Leon will always keep his promise.

5

*P*_{sychic} *Ability and Responsibility*

Louis was asked: *Will I ever develop second sight, and how can I prepare myself?*

As people develop their awareness, as people start to expand their consciousness, this automatically falls into place. It is not something people need to seek or look for or develop. Rather, know that it is coming and that when it comes, it comes little by little; and as the veil is lifted, you have an obligation to use it to help those about you.

Is it good to try contacting spirits through automatic writing?

We do not know what "good" or "bad" is. However, we do not think it is wise. You see, many times when we do this type of thing, we contact what is called the "astral plane." Now, the astral plane is very similar to a railroad station. There are all sorts of individuals milling about, so that if you do get information, it is not reliable. And what does this do to lift your consciousness or make you more aware or put you in touch with any higher reality? We don't really recommend it.

We have a letter here from a lady who apparently has been experiencing automatic writings, and she states: "The spirit apparently is a man who seems to know me very well."

Yes. This woman is contacting an entity, an individual who has been with her many, many lifetimes; and consequently, there is a very deep relation. We do not ordinarily recommend automatic writing because sometimes people tend to pervert it and use it for things that are light and not serious, and they do not use it to develop their insight. However, in this case it seems to be a good thing. We would recommend that this individual keep this going with this person, who is trying to help her; but she must remember that sometimes—even though these people are without their bodies—they are no more effective, informed, or spiritual than they were on the earth plane. Before she gets involved in automatic writing and things of this sort, she must start studying some of the spiritual laws.

Apparently this entity says that he works for God, that he was her husband ten times, and that he is her eternal love.

Yes, but it still does not affect this life's pattern. It is all interesting and titillating and so forth, but in order for this woman to grow and expand, she must study. She must meditate, and she must get a better grasp on what she is dealing with. This woman is good, kind, and loving; she has tried to do good all her life. At times she has been used, because she is so loving and kind. We recommend that she study, learn to meditate, and get a firm, spiritual foundation before she pursues these other things. They are not bad, but they do just act as diversions, and this she does not need.

Is she to be a clairvoyant in this lifetime?

She already is clairvoyant, though not a professional one. She already has certain intuitive awareness; but one does not *try* to be a clairvoyant. One first must learn the natural laws, the spiritual laws, and how they interpenetrate one another. Everyone must have a groundwork, a framework, and build from there; and from this clairvoyance comes.

Is there such a thing as a spiritual adviser?

If you are talking about a master teacher or something of that sort, we do not think this is necessary. However, one does need a person to guide his spiritual path, to tell him to take a look at this or that, try this or that—someone to steer the boat, lead the way. This is very necessary and good; but people do not need someone with a turban, earrings, crystal ball, and some strange name to do this.

What is the reaction of "psi" powers between people? If two or three psychics have predicted the same thing for a person, are they perhaps tuning in on one another?

It is quite possible. The so-called psychic phenomena can be experienced on many levels. If it is experienced near what we would term an intellectual level, then it takes on the fallibilities of intellectuality. But as the psychic or the perceptor perceives into the more abstract levels of consciousness, his accuracy increases because it leaves the atmosphere of the limited earth experience and takes on unlimited ramifications.

The abilities of many psychics are very injured because they become a commodity. It's almost like a machine—you put in a coin and pull a lever and expect an answer—and it takes on a very mechanical ramification which leads to many inaccuracies. But when you go beyond this and start delving into other realms of consciousness, then the answers that come forth take on a universality. They are concerned with principles, with things that have a reality, an eternality about them. From this point of view, they would have accuracy. Most psychics or "perceptors" are forced because of economic and other limitations to work within a very narrow framework, and their work takes on a hit-or-miss atmosphere.

What of responsibility?

Few people realize what responsibility is, and perhaps few can comprehend responsibility in its total essence. There are levels of responsibility as there are levels to almost anything: levels of love, levels of this and that. Everything comes in levels or degrees, including degrees of responsibility. If you take it to its farthest extreme, you actually have responsibility only to yourself; but then there are these minor or degreed responsibilities. These are in the category of Karma, that word battered about so by mystics.

Are there any other responsibilities?

There is responsibility that you assume and there is responsibility that is just part of living, the responsibility of birth.

Is that Karmic?

No, but if I tell you I am going to do something, then that sets up a responsibility; and if I don't do it, then I have a debt there, a minus spot, a black spot in the pattern; and this is Karma.

So the first responsibility is to yourself and all other responsibility is Karmic.

Yes. If you say you are going to do something, for God's sake, do it, come hell or high water; don't say you are going to do something that you are not, because although these are small Karmic debts, when you multiply this by a thousand it becomes a huge thing. One grain of sand is a very small thing, but ten tons of grains of sand can kill you.

All responsibility, then, is responsibility to your self, because your responsibility to yourself is to build up this Karmic reservoir or bank balance.

Right.

Do I have a responsibility to my parents?

Yes, because your parents gave you the opportunity to incarnate and take another step, as many steps as you can, up the ladder, even reach the top. It doesn't matter if you like them or dislike them, you must realize that you do have a responsibility to them, because they provided you with that initial vehicle.

What else about responsibility to my family?

You have a responsibility to your wife, to your children, brothers and sisters—to the other members of your family. You have a responsibility to all people which varies in degree. Toward some you will have a keener, a more intimate responsibility.

How about responsibility to your children?

You have a responsibility for your child's physical, mental, and spiritual health—to help that child as long as the child needs help, until he can make decisions and do things for himself. Once the child reaches the point (which is at a very young age) where he can make decisions, then that responsibility drops off. For example, you have a responsibility to carry the child around until he can walk, to feed him with your hand until he can feed himself, and so on.

How about responsibility to the world?

"I am my brother's keeper." You have a responsibility to be first of all a loving person, to treat all people fairly and equally. Much of this was laid down in the Ten Commandments, which actually are responsibilities.

So many people on this earth complain about things; they don't like the way this or that is done. The moment you say you don't like the way something is done, you have the responsibility to do something about it. If there is something in your life that you do not like, then don't sit around and talk about it—do something about it. Responsibility assumes action of some sort. Many people in this world today toss aside responsibility; but you can't sidestep it. If you have a responsibility of any kind, some day, some way, that is going to have to be taken care of. Why not take care of it now? Many responsibilities are minor in scope and can be taken care of quite easily right away, but if they are allowed to go on, then they become a major responsibility.

There is mental and spiritual responsibility, responsibility to expand your consciousness, to grow. A good question for students of metaphysics to ask themselves is: What have I done today to increase my awareness? If you cannot find something, then that is indeed a lost day.

Many people try to shove all their responsibilities onto somebody else; many people take responsibilities on themselves that really do not belong to them; this is what we call butting in or meddling. My teacher, Leon, once said to me, "Sometimes, Louis, you have to say to yourself that it is none of your damn business."

Responsibility is a matter of awareness, of consciousness. As you become more aware and more evolved, you become more aware of responsibility and take care of things when they need to be taken care of. That is why the spiritually advanced person goes about with such grace, ease, and beauty—he knows his responsibility and he takes care of it.

37

6

The Eternality of the Soul

Recount the creation of souls.

In the beginning there was space, and contained within this space was polarity, unmanifested polarity.

As the various molecules and matter in space began to magnify and attract and repel, planets were formed. Contrary to some beliefs, there are millions and millions of planets—many of which are inhabited. Now as the various bits of matter began slowly to solidify and began to attract and repel one another, there was set up a force field. The force field took on a personality, perhaps we should say identity.

In essence, there is one soul, and all things are but fragments or parts of that soul, that spirit.

As aeons and aeons of time passed, there began a progression of changes. The first kingdom was the mineral kingdom. Next, as the molecules started re-forming, the plant kingdom came into consideration, then the lower animal kingdom. When the human being came into existence, there was a refinement of identification.

Many men and women like to think that there was some creator entity that had a great, large pot of soul substance, who formed all the individual souls and sent them forth, but it is not so. Soul growth or soul identification or soul essence is a matter of refinement, restructuring.

In essence, soul and God are one. The soul is a thing that man likes to identify with and say, "It is my soul." Strangely enough, nothing belongs to anyone. Man likes to think that he possesses, but this concept is a fallacy. All is part of the One. Individualized, yes; compartmentalized, yes; but we are all a portion of what we choose to call the Mother-Father Principle.

Was there really a beginning?

Not really, but there was a time when man went from the unmanifested to the manifested, if you choose to call that a beginning. There was a beginning of manifestation, but everything has always been in an unmanifested state.

7

How to Enter Meditative Silence and Find Union with God

Louis: Meditation is very good. However, it is not complete in itself. One needs more than meditation. It is as if one asked, "Should I have fruit in my diet?" Yes, one should have fruit, but he should have a variety of proper foods.

It is the same with the spiritual diet. Meditation is a very important part of that spiritual diet, but there are other considerations that enter into the picture. One needs to study; one needs to relate to other people; one needs to apply his studies; and one needs to meditate, as well. But man needs all these things in a pattern of balance.

One will find as he practices meditation and delves in philosophy that many doors will open to him. He will gain a completely new way of looking at life and his world, present and past. He will be able to release many of the things in the past and become more involved in the Now. This is good, for one's life will then take on a real purpose. It will take on a meaning and a substance that it didn't have before. But remember always that the great key lies in application. It is important to seek and to find, but then one must use what has been found. He must learn to become one with that new consciousness.

To make reality awareness function within you, it is necessary to expand your consciousness and to make your life, not an existence, but a life that is alive and vibrant and thrilling. Each moment that we are alive should be an exciting experience, not a dull routine where we say, "Oh, must I face another day," but each moment should be thrilling and exciting. Once we are aware, truly aware, this begins to occur.

You can spend hours and days studying, but if you do not apply these studies, these truths, these principles into your everyday life, they become worthless. When you begin to apply that which is being presented to you, it will become more valuable to you than all the treasures in the world. You shall more fully understand the meaning of the statement, "As ye sow, so shall ye reap." As you proceed with these studies, you will find that each man truly shapes his destiny . . . and it is shaped by the thought mechanism. If you want a constructive world, you must start with constructive thoughts. *Everything* begins with a thought—every deed, every action. Constructive thoughts build a constructive world: *Your World!*

How do you think? Are your thoughts constructive or destructive? You have seen many persons who are forever going to do this or forever going to do that, but they can't do this or that because they have arthritis or it is raining or it is cold or there is not time. Nothing gets done.

Excuses are mental, physical, and spiritual weaknesses. They are loopholes through which we slip to avoid realities. You cannot resort to a passive expression and expect to reap the full force of the great cosmic God-Power. Realize your excuses, know when they occur, and know why they occur. Be aware of them.

When you find yourself in the mood to make excuses, stop short in your mental action and be honest. The action will require discipline to break the negative habit, but the moment the correction is made in your thinking, your conscious mind will become more in tune with the oneness of God that permeates all creation.

There are two methods of reaching or acquiring your potential—meditation and study.

Most people think that meditation is something mysterious, something mystical. They think in terms of trances and all sorts of weird mumbo-jumbo. And yet, meditation can be the most valuable tool to help you achieve expanded awareness, because it helps you to lay aside the conscious reality and enter into true reality.

There are many types of meditation, and we find them all to have merit. First of all, you should set a time when you want to meditate. At the Louis Foundation we meditate each evening at 10:00 o'clock. You may join us in this meditation and take advantage of the vibrational force field that is created each evening.

To meditate, sit erect, with the spine straight, both feet placed upon the floor, hands on the lap. Do not recline, but sit up straight. Close your eyes.

Start to *concentrate* on something, bring all your thoughts into focus. Concentrate on one thing, anything, but one thing. After a few moments, *contemplate* something you think to be beautiful or holy or good or fine—something that lifts you up. It could be a flower, a person, or a color. Try to feel this thing you are contemplating. If, for example, you contemplate a rose, try to feel like that rose. Feel like its structure. Realize its fragrance. Be aware of its beauty.

After you have gone through the process of focusing and feeling, *release* and let go, little by little, until you become a void or a nothing. Empty the cup so the cup can be filled.

Many students ask how long to meditate. It does not really matter. It can be three minutes or three hours. Meditate until you feel that it is time to cease. Usually a half-hour is sufficient for the beginning student, an hour for more progressed students.

Meditation, then, is a process of *concentration, contemplation,* and *release.* This is the abstract or intuitive method of reaching self-awareness.

Through study—the tangible or intellectual approach—self-awareness can also be attained. Both meditation and study are necessary for spiritual growth. They provide the keys for unlocking spiritual truths. Both are needed for balance.

Application of these two methods is as important as the methods themselves. All the meditation and study in the world will be of little value unless that which is acquired becomes an integral part of your daily life.

It can be said that a person's *attitude* depends on his *attitude*. In other words, if a student wishes to grow, to expand, to climb the ladder of awareness, he must have the proper attitude.

Begin your development by determining to improve your attitude. You improve your thinking by improving your attitude. "As a man thinketh, so he is." Good attitude promotes good thinking, and the result will be a good person, an aware person.

Not only does attitude influence your thought pattern, but it affects your entire behavior pattern as well. Your outward behavior pattern is in actuality a reaction to your inward attitude. If you change your attitude, you will change your behavior pattern, your entire structure within and without. This is basically how you can change your whole life. It presents a new structure, a new set of laws, a new set of principles. You can destroy outward constructive motion by a negative attitude of the mind. Be positive.

Even if you have a positive attitude, positive action or constructive motion can still be destroyed if the motive is not pure. Examine your real motive behind your thought-motion. If you have negative motive and a positive attitude, all the positive action in the world is not really going to accomplish anything. A positive attitude and a positive motive are both necessary to expand.

Prior to beginning any meditation you should prepare yourself both mentally and physically, so that you can receive spirituality. First, take a hot bath to cleanse the physical body and to relax it. Next, garb yourself in loose attire of some sort. Women may wear something of the muu-muu variety and the men, anything that is comfortable. It really doesn't matter what you wear, but the clothing should be loose. The garments that you wear for meditation should be worn for meditation purposes *only;* and it is also best never to wear any animal products on your body during meditation, such as wool, leather, etc.

Zen meditation is to be practiced alone, and the procedure is as follows:

Sit upon the floor facing a bare wall about twenty inches away. The wall should be white, and you should stare at a dot approximately the size of a quarter placed upon that wall. The dot can be of any color, but it should be at eye level. Stare at the dot, concentrate and contemplate. Finally, close your eyes and remove yourself from the sensory reality. Release.

Zen meditation has been used successfully for many thousands of years. As is true with any form of Oriental philosophy, two basic premises prevail. First, spiritual discipline; second, simplicity. We feel that there is merit to both these aspects, and we should incorporate these premises into our daily lives. Generally, we of the Western world tend to clutter that which we're involved in, and it would behoove us to heed the words of the Zen master as he talks to his student; "Simplify, simplify, simplify, and simplify some more." If we look realistically upon the world around us, cannot it all be simplified?

Color meditation was developed in the late eighteenth century by those involved in various color societies of England. Color meditation is very good for those who think or relate in terms of symbols or visual pictures, and it is a particularly good meditation for those who have acute visual awareness.

Color meditation may be combined with music meditation and may be practiced alone or in groups. Assume a comfortable meditation position and close your eyes. Concentrate on a situation wherein you can transcend through a color media, such as stairsteps painted different colors, a garden with different colored flowers, a wallpaper, etc.

First imagine a red color. See and feel the color. Then imagine an orange color, yellow, green, blue, indigo, and violet. Concentrate on each color individually for a few moments until you have conceptualized all seven colors. Then, transcend the body, visualize white, and release into cosmic consciousness.

Mandala meditation comes from various forms of Indian philosophies. The concept behind it is for the student to lose himself in the somewhat complicated design structure of the mandala; in so doing, he will find it easier to release other thought patterns. This is an individual meditation technique.

With colored pencils, chalk, or crayon, color a design according to your inner awareness. Make the colors as intense or dull or pastel as you desire. Color it until you feel good with it. Then, place it on a wall, as in the Zen meditation instructions, and concentrate.

In the Zen meditation, however, you were asked to concentrate and contemplate upon a dot. Here you are asked to concentrate and contemplate upon an entire picture. So, let your eyes *wander* over the entire picture; notice each specific part of the coloring. Close your eyes, release.

The use of music in conjunction with meditation knows no geographical origin, and it can be traced almost to the dawn of civilization. Because music is an abstract expression, one meditating with music can many times more easily overcome three-dimensional imagery. Music helps to liberate and transcend the physical plane and may be used either individually or in a group.

It's interesting to note that during meditation, the higher three chakras vibrate. They are receptive and they are "in tune." Uplifting music helps to set these three zones into motion, whereas other types of music vibrate the lower three zones or chakras, and prohibit the higher three zones from functioning. (Each set of three chakras forms a triangle and these two triangles, when placed together, form the Star of David.) The center chakra does not vibrate with either group, but rather acts as a buffer and a transition between the two.

To experience music meditation, sit quietly and listen to music that moves you emotionally. Concentrate and contemplate this music so that when it has ended you will be able to enter the nonphysical realm by transcending through the quiet. Let the music act as a vehicle to spring you into cosmic consciousness.

Classical music is the most beneficial and uplifting of all

46

music. Avoid using modern contemporary music for meditation purposes, for it serves to disintegrate or to pull apart. This is the reason that the younger generation of today enjoys this music, for it tends to pull them apart from that which is established. Most people have too much of this "pulling apart" as it is; and this type of music has no place in meditation. This serves to vibrate only the lower chakras, and prohibits the upper three chakras from functioning.

The very old technique of moving meditation has been revived by various Oriental schools of philosophy and is best experienced if a person meditating in this manner wears a garment that is very, very loose.

Stand comfortably. Close your eyes and relax. Concentrate on your body and be aware of your arms, your legs, your torso, your entire physical being. Slowly begin to move your arms. Contemplate your arms moving and notice how they swing. Feel the muscles move. Realize that your body and your movement is a part of God. The body is a temple of God. Your body is the body of God. Release and be at one with God.

You may want to walk slowly or move around the room a bit. Sometimes moving meditation can be combined with music meditation, but we would recommend that you experience moving meditation by yourself a few times without the music. Later, use Indian music, such as sitar selections. Such music is good for this combination because it is slow and rhythmic.

Many students of Eastern philosophy consider the "OM" to be *the* perfect sound, and they refer to it as the sound of perfection beyond perfection. You will find that in using this sound in meditation a very strong vibrational force field is built up. You will find also that it helps to lift you to a higher level of consciousness.

Sit erect in the usual meditation position and gently sing or hum the word "OM" in a monotone voice. Stretch the word out so that it requires 15 seconds, more or less, to pronounce it. Pronounce first the long "O" sound and stretch it out. Next pronounce the soft "M" sound and draw it out. Place equal emphasis on each letter and let the OM sound flow in a steady monotonish, humming-like sound. Don't force it; rather relax and let it flow. It doesn't matter what tone you use to pronounce the word; however, the D sound directly above middle C seems to have the best vibration for this type of meditation.

As you first begin to pronounce the sounds, concentrate on the sounds themselves and listen to your voice. After two or three OMs, feel the sound and notice how it vibrates throughout your entire physical body. After this concentration and contemplation, finally let go, release. Be quiet and dissolve into universal consciousness. The OM represents the perfect sound or the God sound, and it acts as a vehicle to transcend you upward.

Many students prefer to meditate with their own private sound, a sound that immediately triggers them into deep meditation. All sounds are a form of the concentration and contemplation process and help to transcend the self from the manifested into the unmanifested.

All meditations are transcendental, as all meditation procedures have as their objective the transcending from the physical to the nonphysical. You see, the purpose of meditation is too often lost because of all the conjecturing and worry about the procedures of the act of meditation itself. Few people realize that the purpose of meditation is to make the whole life a meditation. You should always be "tuned on" and "tuned in," as the teenagers today would state. You should not have to resort to allowing only a few minutes a day to meditate to get "there," but you should rather always *be there.* All meditations are transcendental, but if the OM sound, or your own private sound helps you to reach a high state of consciousness easily, then that is the method we would recommend for you.

The blanket meditation technique was developed by some of the early-day researchers in the field of psychoanalysis. Their theory was that the blanket represented the womb, and thus the person felt secure or safe therein. This "fetal sac" psychologically freed the individual from his present hang-ups by offering him a temporary protection from the outside world. It is interesting to note that the American Indian uses this same technique.

Sit on a large blanket. Get comfortable. Cover yourself up completely. This procedure is best practiced in the nude.

Basically, all the various methods of meditation are processes of "letting go and letting God." Meditation is like lighting the pilot light on a stove. It maintains a steady flame that can blend itself into many facets of the thing we call life.

Some questions on meditation which were asked of the Source:

What is the strange sensation that I feel in my forehead when I've started meditation?

This is what is referred to as the "third eye." This center is opening, expanding in you. You are a very intuitive person, but you hide it. You seem afraid of it. You know these abilities lie latent within you, but you keep asking yourself, "What if I did open up completely? Could I handle it?" The answer is *yes*.

Is our present method of transcendental meditation the most appropriate method for our group to use? Are we making progress with it? Will any of us reach Cosmic Consciousness in this lifetime?

The method is good. It has raised your level of consciousness. You will yet delve into other vistas, but this method of meditation has been almost like an elevator, in that you have gone up another level. However, there are yet many floors to transcend, and you shall. Cosmic Consciousness is within the grasp of all. You have already known Cosmic Consciousness for brief, fractional moments. The secret is to sustain those moments into minutes, hours, years—into a lifetime.

How can I best serve my Father in heaven through meditation?

Your Father is not in heaven, he is within you. If you expand your consciousness, your awareness, you will serve the Father within.

When I pray, a strange phenomenon occurs. Could you explain this to me?

This is not really a phenomenon. You see, when one prays, he becomes more God-Realized, more God-Aware, more God-Attuned; consequently, there is a speeding up of vibration, a raising of vibrational frequencies, and things begin to happen. They are not mysterious, unreal, or phenomenal—they are very real.

8

Making the Laws of Action Meaningful

A lady wrote to Louis:

I feel I am behind a veil and have been in a mental prison for such a long time.

It's because you have failed to realize your potential. You are really none of the things you have told yourself you are. You are actually a very beautiful person, a very shining person with many potentialities and abilities; but covering these are fears and doubts and anxieties. You constantly say, "Who am I? . . little me . . . I can't do this and I can't do that." But you can; you can have a new life with a new attitude.

This is your key: Your attitude, and your feeling of expectancy. Expect beauty, and there will be beauty. Expect wonderful things to happen, and they will. Do not look down, look up.

We know that you have considered suicide many times, but this is not your answer. The answer is to live, not to die; to grow, not to stagnate; to smile, not to cry. Think upon these things, and this very day can mark a new chapter in your life, a chapter filled with wonderful things, happy things. This is what it can be, but you must make it so.

You are intelligent, attractive, with many abilities. You say to yourself, "What abilities do I have?" You have many, many; but you have allowed them to get rusty. You've put them away as if they were some worthless toys. Reshape your life; reshape your destiny. Walk upright, not bent over. It will take some doing; it will not come easy. It is much easier to walk in a rut than to climb out and walk an uncharted course; but this you must do, so prepare for it. Get ready, and the days ahead will truly be filled with love and wonder and beauty. Yours can be a most happy life, a life filled with days that seem to bubble into eternity. So look not upon the yesterdays, look not upon the unhappy things, but look upon that which you are yet to manifest, and you shall have a life fulfilled.

Attitude is important, then?

Attitude is the powerhouse. So many students of metaphysics, striving to grow, to expand, to increase their awareness, wonder why they fail. They run about and attend lectures; they read books; they meditate when it is convenient; and yet all these motions and utterances seem to add up to other confusions. If they were to sit down and perform what I call a spiritual introspection—to analyze their thought structure, their feeling structure, their motion structure—they would find that attitude is of primary importance. It is the sperm, the seed, the very first essential motion.

What kinds of attitudes are there?

Attitude can be of three types. It can be positive or constructive; it can be a nothing, a void; or it can be destructive. Unfortunately, many people have the in-between attitude; they are neither negative nor positive. They wonder why their life is continuously on a plateau, why it doesn't go up or go down, and why it is very unexciting, very blah. Many, many people are caught in the psychological-spiritual blahs, and it is because of their attitude.

What does attitude mean, then?

Attitude means one's feeling—and I am not talking about peripheral feeling or surface feeling. I am talking about the feeling that permeates the totality: How you feel about things from the intellectual level, from all levels. How *do* you feel? Do you feel good; do you feel right; do you feel excited; do you feel lifted? Attitude sets the rhythmic pattern for anything in which you are involved. If a person has no feelings, if he doesn't care what is going to happen—nothing happens. The caring triggers off the action.

Are you saying that everything begins with a thought?

Yes. If this thought is of a positive, dynamic, constructive, uplifting nature, then anything that is conceived in that thought is going to grow and bloom and have a fantastic harvest. It is very akin to planting a garden: If we plant dead seeds in our garden, then nothing takes place; there is no harvest. But if we plant live, vibrant seeds with care, then the harvest is very abundant. People do not have abundance in their lives on many levels—sociological, environmental, material, spiritual. This is why it behooves us to send forth from this powerhouse within our consciousness the very highest, the very best.

Quite frequently I have heard someone state, "I am going to apply for a job, but I don't really think I am going to get it." You see, this was canceled out, because of the attitude, the thought: "I don't think I am going to get it." Immediately there has been a barrier set up. And who set it up but the person himself? "I don't think I can do this or that" is a destructive, negative type of thinking.

We also have the people who have no viewpoints, no thoughts about anything: "I don't know this; I have no feeling on this; I have no expression. . . ."

Man comes into life to express, not in a placid undynamic way, but to be a dynamic moving vehicle. After all, man is a bit of God, a bit of the Magnificence. He comes into this life to glow. This is the auric glow—to expand, to grow, to share, to give, to live, and not just to exist.

But how can you live if you do not have a living attitude?

If we have a positive, constructive attitude toward ourselves and our world, then nothing is denied us; it is all there awaiting us. God never says no. God does not limit—only man says no, and he says it with this thing called attitude.

How can we change our attitude? By sitting down and doing a self-analysis, a spiritual introspection, looking with very candid eyes at the situation. *Ask:* How am I approaching it? What am I broadcasting? What is coming forth from my powerhouse? Am I sending out vibrations of expectancy, of joy? Am I a dynamic, throbbing, exciting person? Exciting people *meet* exciting people, joyful people meet joyful people, because there is a magnetism involved. The thoughts we send out are very magnetic and draw into us exactly what is sent forth.

About how much of the world is a zero?

Unfortunately, a great percentage of the people in the world are zeroes; they sit undirected.

You mean they add very little to the life stream.

They neither add nor subtract; they just are sort of blobs of nothing. They exist; they do not live. Perhaps ten percent at most of the people of the world are really living, because living is *giving.* The people that are giving to the world are the people who are living. The people who say, "Well, I have nothing to give," or "I can't do this," who sit there and bemoan their fate, who talk about *"they"* out there—*"they* did this and *they* did that"—these are your "zero people." They never have an opinion on anything; they never have an idea; they just sit there—and they are very vulnerable.

They may have opinions and ideas, but they do very little about them?

Yes, they may have opinions or ideas, but they never act upon them. You must have action in your life, and behind the action there must be positive thought. Positive thought, coupled with positive action, produces positive results.

To get out of the minus, or the zero category and into the plus category, one must have positive thoughts and then act upon these thoughts in a positive way?

Yes. If you are dissatisfied with yourself, sit down and survey all that you are unhappy with in your life; consider what you are doing about it. Then the results take place. This is a very simple thing, but it works.

How does all this relate to the growth of the individual?

With the positive, living person, there is growth. You have a living plant, and it is growing, getting new leaves and new flowers. The *existing* plant just sort of sits there, gathering dust.

Is this the only way in which growth can take place?

Yes, you must have a positive, constructive attitude, or no growth can take place.

Is growth one reason that we come to earth?

This is the *only* reason why we come to earth.

Then all growth begins with a positive thought, followed by a positive action. This is the only way in which growth can take place. The reason we come to earth is to grow, and the earth is the only place where we may grow.

Exactly! This is part of the destiny of man. If people will assess their situations, formulate some positive thoughts, then follow them with some positive actions, theirs will become very positive, living, growing, very joyous lives. "Your altitude depends upon your attitude." If you want to climb upon the mountain and reach high altitudes, you must have high attitudes.

Can you change your attitude or your thought pattern in a moment, or is it something that takes a while to practice and to build up?

Little by little, I think. If one has been in a very negative rut, one must make small gains in order to make larger ones. But any journey starts with a step. You start where you are, re-assess the situation, and start changing your thinking and actions. Then little by little—but in less time than you might think—you can get out of horrible ruts and horrible situations. I have seen people change their whole lives in a matter of a few days.

Are assumptions related to attitudes?

Assumptions can be a very dangerous form of thought; and while they are practiced by everyone, they usually are of a negative nature. You see, that which you assume is placed in motion so that eventually it becomes a part of you and a part of your reality. If you assume that which is a part of God-reality or the eternal reality, then this goodness will become a part of you and your reality. However, if you assume that which exists in the world of deterioration, then this will become a part of you and your reality.

As an example, many parents tell their children that if they eat this or eat that, they will become ill. And if the children eat these things, then they do become ill because they assume that they will. The parents' negative assumptions infect the children with negative assumptions. As these assumptions are placed into motion, they become a part of the child, whether they be positive or negative. Do you know that you could eat anything and not become ill if you only assumed that you could? You could live to be 500 years old if you only assumed that you could live to be that age.

Are there other dangers?

Assumptions can also be dangerous because you are not always aware that you are assuming. Assumptions can be either conscious or subconscious, and your subconscious mind may be playing tricks on you. As an example, do you purchase automobile insurance? If you do—and most people have automobile insurance—do you know that you are assuming that you will have an accident? And you will, if you place that assumption in motion! Your subconscious mind is tricking you into a very negative assumption. You assume so many things every day of a negative nature, because you are not fully aware. However, anything that you assume, whether you are totally aware of it or not, will become part of your reality.

Assumptions can also be dangerous because they have the power and influence to shape your destiny. Faith, which is usually a positive assumption, is a good example.

Remember: That which you assume is brought back to you; you have the power to create something in your reality that may not already exist. You can create something in your reality that may have previously existed only in God-reality. Man must live by grace. He must assume the constant presence of God.

Assume and concern yourself only with that which you *know*, not with that which you know *about*. It is not necessary to assume anything of the physical world. As you become more aware, it will not be necessary to assume anything in the nonphysical world either.

You see, as you know—and know that you know—then

assumptions will cease and you *will* know, *truly know!* That which you know will be true knowledge and will be most beautiful. You will, therefore, not bring anything into your reality that is not of God-reality, for you will not be assuming anything that is non-eternal. That which is eternal, you will already have brought into your reality. That which you *know,* you bring into your reality.

Since we all assume, then let us assume that which is true, beautiful, real, positive, eternal. Assume that your life is going to be beautiful. It is a part of reality and a part of you. Assume each day is going to be the same way—a wonderful, wonderful day. Every week and every year is built upon days. Soon you will have a beautiful constructive life.

The clock ticks the seconds away; your awareness draws nearer and nearer; and your adventure in God's adorning of his handicraft approaches your sparkling self, your realized self.

Re-program your conscious mind by extracting the *minuses* and replacing them with *pluses.* Assume only the positive. Psychiatrists may say that you are living in a dream world, but that is what was said about Luther Burbank, Thomas Edison, and most of the outstanding creative pace-setters. They assumed only that which is positive, and they accomplished the "so-called" impossible. They assumed only that which is real, and they brought it into their reality. *So can you!*

9

The Dynamic Pattern of All Things

The first obstacle that must be removed from man's thinking when he views the Cosmos is the concept of limitation. Most human beings constantly use some sort of measuring device for everything. If you are to understand the manifestation, or that which lies behind and is not manifested, you must start thinking in terms of an unlimited pattern.

Second, you must understand that everything is linked with something else. True, there are many levels to manifestation and many levels of that which is not manifested. Think of these levels as stairsteps; are not stairsteps joined together? They are not separate from one another, but form a continuum.

Part of the dynamics of the manifested world has to do with rhythms—not rhythms like music, although that is related— you might call it "rate" or "speed," but basically, it is a rhythm. As the rhythm becomes more intense, the world of the manifested becomes the world of the unmanifested.

The world of the manifested and the unmanifested are the same; only many men cannot perceive them so. Their eyes are limited to a certain spectrum, a certain pattern. Their hearing, their feeling is all limited. If we were to remove this limitation, then there would truly be just one world.

For clarification, how would you define "unmanifested" and "manifested"?

Unmanifested things have a high rate of vibration. As that vibration is slowed down, things become manifested; but they are the same.

Are manifested things three-dimensional?

Yes.

Are unmanifested things three-dimensional?

Yes and no. There is just *a* dimension. Dimensions are just stairsteps. The fourth dimension is connected to the third and the fifth, and so on.

Can you perceive the unmanifested with your eyes?

Yes; some do . . . a very small number. Man recognizes a disappearing point, but that doesn't mean there really is such a point. Are not water, ice, and steam the same thing? It is the same with everything else. When steam becomes water and water becomes ice, the molecular action slows down; the rhythm has slowed down; it is cold. As the molecular pattern or rhythm changes, the other forms change; but they are the same thing in essence. You can apply this principle to everything.

Is it necessary to understand this unmanifested aspect?

It is only necessary to understand yourself—then these things of which you are a part will be understood as well. There is a manifested aspect of you and an unmanifested; but, in essence, you are unlimited. You are limited only by that which you impose upon yourself.

Would you say that ideas are an unmanifested aspect of an action?

Yes, ideas or inspirations are like the "steam." As the rhythm changes, they may be brought into certain action patterns.

Do all things exist in this "steam" form before they exist in more tangible form?

Yes, these are one and the same—only it is much easier to understand an orange, say, than it is to understand an orange *seed.* If you could really be aware of the seed, you would be aware of the fruit at the same time. Again, there is a change of rhythm. Even time is a rhythm.

Does man exist in a higher vibratory state before coming to this plane?

Yes, he is in what is called "the world of the spirit"— although this is a misnomer because spirit has to do with collection, rather than with individuality.

And as man ends his existence on this earth plane, are his vibrations increased into the unmanifested state?

Yes, depending upon how much he has grown in, or raised, his consciousness; how "fine the particles" are; how intense the rhythm.

So his rhythm in the unmanifested state, upon completion of a life cycle, will be somewhat different from that at the beginning of a life cycle?

Yes.

What is the ultimate?

To be At-One-With. Man is now Separate-From.

It would seem to me that you're always At-One-With when you're not in the manifested state.

Yes, on some level. All stairsteps are not the top step.

It is easy to relate this to the importance of thought or ideas—and perhaps to the thought behind the thought. As it is stated in the Bible, "Ye are what ye think ye are. . . ."

"As a man thinketh, so he is." The more we can break down the gates of limitation, the more man can grow and expand and reach greater awareness.

If you put a plant in a very tiny pot, the roots can go just so far. Most people plant themselves into very tiny pots. If there were such a thing as "sin" or "evil" (which there is not), we could label this thing "limitation." Man comes into an earth experience to grow—that is *the* reason he is here—yet he immediately plants himself into the smallest pot he can find and then complains because nothing happens.

Would it be correct to say that life is man's opportunity to raise his vibrations?

Yes, or to expand his consciousness or awareness. Life is not limited, though, to the manifested world.

If man recognizes the disappearing point, is the object of raising one's awareness to do away with the disappearing point?

Yes, to go beyond it. Look at a lifetime, look at any cluster of human beings. Listen to them, feel them, watch their actions. They are constantly recognizing limitations.

If we are serious about knowing ourselves, and if we are concerned about raising the vibratory pattern and working at it, how can we know we are succeeding?

By your life. If you are succeeding, there will be joy; perhaps not happiness, but joy. If you are succeeding, you are giving on many levels; and there will be a feeling of success, a feeling of Oneness-With. Man talks constantly about the Source, yet he works so diligently to separate himself from it.

The dynamic key to understanding this supposed "phenomenon" of manifestation is understanding the rhythm. Everything has a rhythm which you can relate to molecular activity. There's always a rhythm involved, a rhythm of life. When man starts truly to understand these rhythms, that everything is part of one rhythm, then he will understand the Universe; he will find that he *is* the Universe.

10

How to Shape Your Destiny

What is my destiny upon this earth?

You came to this earth plane, first, to seek self-awareness, self-knowledge, realization; and in acquiring this, it is your destiny to pass these bits of wisdom on to others. Not only are you to light the light within yourself, but in others as well.

How can I do this? By first becoming more aware?

First, seek self-awareness; when that has been established, it will act as a magnet. People will be drawn to you. As they come, you have a duty and an obligation to help them. Herein lies your work for days ahead.

Do we ask to be born?

Yes, and you choose your parents and the other situations about you.

Is there a reason why one chooses his parents?

Yes: They have the right chemical and psychological make-up for what is necessary for one's mission.

Can you have more than one mission in a lifetime?

There is one mission, but it has various facets. As, for instance, if you have a "mission" to the grocery store, while

63

there you may purchase bread, butter, and so forth; stop and talk to a friend; or any of a number of things.

If we begin as a perfected soul and end as a perfected soul, why the trip in between?

You come as a drop and you end as an ocean. You come as a tiny flame and you end as a bonfire.

How can we fulfill our mission if we don't know what that mission is?

The important thing is to *live* the moment, to *live* each day, to *know* and to *express* the perfection within you. As you do this, you will know your mission.

What should I be doing in this life to further my spirit and soul?

You need to meditate, to study, to get involved with the real you, which you have yet to find. You have become very involved with surface things, but you need to discover that below this surface there is a spiritual you, a soul, with which you must get acquainted. It cannot be done in an hour or a day, but if you delve into study and meditate, it will come. Many of your frustrations, your doubts and fears, will pass away. Your attitudes and expression of life will become more positive, more expansive. Good things will come about, because you'll be expecting them.

What can I do to create a better life for those around me and myself?

Try to be more loving, both physically and psychologically. Get yourself organized. Express this love that is within you. Don't be afraid to hug and kiss. Be loving. This is the most important thing you can share with others.

Why am I denied what I would like most?

You need not be denied these things. You need only to conceive yourself in this situation, to believe you can be in it, then you will achieve it. You need to go about things in a more systematic way. You tend to be a bit haphazard, a bit sporadic, and a bit negative. At times you tend to think: "All these wonderful things are out there, but they are not mine. I can't have them. I want them, but I don't have what it takes to get them." This is where you're mistaken. You have within you all the keys, all it takes. You simply must apply them systematically.

Nothing is denied you. Man only denies himself. When he stops denying himself, then truly the Kingdom of Heaven is his. Remember these things, and do not take them lightly. Apply them, and watch the wonderful things that will come into your life. You will see the change of changes, the miracle of miracles: Yourself changing from a little person into a big person—and it can happen rapidly if you will let it.

Doesn't the butterfly start out imprisoned in a cocoon, then break loose and fly? You are in the cocoon right now. You need to break loose, to fly, to soar. It is so easy—so easy; and yet, as we speak to you, you keep saying, "It's so hard, so hard; it's impossible." Don't you know these words are crucifying you? You do not have to accept that which *is,* only that which will be. If you accept that which is beautiful, your life is beautiful. Reject these other things. Reject them in your thoughts, in your deeds. Accept only the wonderful, uplifting, beautiful things; make them a part of your life, and you will grow.

Can you tell us how we can better ourselves spiritually?

Man becomes more spiritual as he becomes more aware of the principles and structure of life. If you close your eyes, you can see very little; if you slowly open your eyes, you can see a bit more. If you open the lids of your eyes completely, then you are able to see and have vision. As you become more and more aware, as you start to open your spiritual awareness, you gain new insights, you expand your horizon to raise your consciousness.

Is a factor that leads to expanding our awareness or consciousness something termed "Letting ourselves go?"

Yes—"Let go and let God." You see, when man relies upon man, upon the facade, upon that only which he can touch and feel, then very shortly he becomes quite lost. As man starts to look at the total picture, he gains new insight.

How does one really let himself go, really express himself as he feels? Why do we hold back? Is it from fear?

When man holds back, he is afraid of what those about him

65

will think. It does not really matter what anyone thinks. Man holds back because he is afraid to let go and express that which is in him. You all must one day, though.

Louis: We all come together to learn. How do we learn? Basically by changing our structure, our intangible structure. There is a design and a structure to the manifested and unmanifested universe, as there is to all things and to all situations. As we learn, and as we put to use what we learn, we are changing our design and our structure.

It is much like a large ocean tanker. Out on the seas there are tremendous vehicles which transport oil and other materials from one country to another. When these vehicles are required to change course, they do not simply stop, change direction, and begin a new course immediately. Sometimes, because of their size and their load, it may take up to five miles to bring the vehicle to a stop, and nearly a half hour will have transpired.

So it is with the human being. The greater the load and the faster the speed, the longer it takes to change direction. We must first bring ourselves to a stop, a complete stop. We must change our direction and aim ourselves the proper way. We must begin on our new course. It is a constant "putting into practice" of the materials that you have learned that changes the course of your ship and, in turn, changes the structure. You see, these things do not happen overnight. We must slow down, change, then proceed.

Once your direction has been altered, once you have slowed down and changed, tremendous growth can begin to take place. The slowing down is the tearing apart of an old pattern and permitting a new pattern to emerge. A new structure comes into focus when the path becomes unobstructed. This is what is happening now. You are becoming more in tune with the real. Now that you have stopped and changed directions and committed yourself, tremendous things can take place.

In order for man to comprehend his spiritual self, he must first comprehend his physical self. Man has a consciousness, the thoughts of which he can control in any manner he desires.

He can occupy his consciousness with his problems, his work, his family, or whatever. But as man begins to expand, he realizes that there is more than just the world that he has been experiencing. There is another world that gives credence and meaning to the physical world. As man begins to experience this other world, his consciousness becomes expanded.

One of the first realizations is that man, physical man, has an unlimited potential. He can do anything that has been done or that he desires to do. This is a marvelous revelation, because even though he is in a physical body, he is not limited. As man realizes this, first intellectually and finally from a point of view of totality, from within, he grows.

A serious student of metaphysics understands why meditation is so vitally important for the development and growth of his person. Meditation represents one side of his growth pattern, and study represents the other. It is this principle of plus-minus, his-her, yin-yang, masculine-feminine, or positive-negative that helps to complete the development of the polarized individual. Through study man can understand intellectually; by meditating, he understands intuitively. One is the expansion of the outward experience, the other is the expansion of the inward experience. Both are needed for total development. One cannot develop merely physically or only spiritually; these aspects must be unified, become one. This is what is lacking in many metaphysical studies. There is too much emphasis placed on either study or meditation. Both are necessary for total growth.

The serious student in metaphysics will consciously strive to maintain a positive attitude toward all things. He will see the "bright" side even in an "impossible" situation. He will realize that there is good in all things, and he will see God in all things and situations. He will approach each situation with expectation. A compelling search for truth will be his. As a student comprehends both intuitively and intellectually that for total growth to be experienced he must drop his negative pattern and supplant it with a positive pattern, then the once "impossible" will become "possible." Negative thoughts and assumptions hinder man's growth and hinder truth from becoming an

67

integral part of one's totality. They short-circuit. If one must assume, he should assume only that which is real and true and beautiful. There is no room in man's consciousness for negative thoughts or assumptions.

Positive assumptions can bring beauty into one's life pattern. You feel this beauty inwardly. If you concentrate on something harmonious, concentrate so strongly that it becomes a part of your vibrational pattern. If you can actually see and feel this thing, then you will be able to experience it. Man has the ability to bring anything into his reality. Remember, God always says yes.

As man expands and as he becomes more aware, he automatically will assume a greater role in the world about him. His responsibilities will increase because he will be more in tune with the universal consciousness and he will be expected to perform more in accordance with this attunement. Each person has a responsibility for himself, for his family, and for others. But now his responsibility has increased, and the role of responsibility should be comprehended. In every meeting, in every situation, in every act of any kind, there is a Karmic overtone and hence an underlying responsibility, whether it is obvious or not. As man expresses truth and as it becomes an integral part of his personality, his responsibility in any given situation, no matter how great or how small, will be increased.

Through careful examination one can now comprehend that everything has an order and everything is necessary and has its position. It is for the student to realize the place of anything and everything and to take on new regard for the unobtrusive or minute. There has been nothing created out of accident, and everything is related to us. Even man's "electrical system" is a thing of beauty and of grand design. Not only does it have a design and structure that is invisible, but it resembles the Universe on a smaller scale. So it is with everything.

It is a wonderful revelation when one can comprehend, even intellectually, that "God is everywhere." As this concept is absorbed into the totality, man's vibrational pattern is increased. Some of our problems of today result from the pious churchgoer who condemns those who do not take active part in "religion." More often than not, however, this same individual leaves God in the church on Sunday, and returns at his convenience whenever he feels the need of a spiritual environment. This individual dies the same way he was born, with little expanded consciousness but great criticism for those who do not participate in the "thing to do." God is in the church, the pages of a novel, a twenty-dollar bill, a football, or a raging storm. All is composed of the same and the same is everywhere in equal amounts. *Everything is an expression of God!*

11

*H*umility

Louis: Humility is additive, not subtractive; it is a plus, not a minus. This is the first consideration. The origin of the word means "to worship"—not as it is known in the twentieth century between ten and eleven each Sunday morning, but worship as a way of life. You see, then, that the word has gone many, many degrees off course.

What about the phrase "humble pie"? That seems to have a negative connotation.

It means "partaking in the feast of life"; it has nothing to do with pie or with eating, as we understand eating or consuming, It has to do with blending or flowing.

Can one be humble and still be proud?

Yes, if you are truly humble and know that you are truly a portion of the Living God. If you are proud of that fact—and you know it is a fact within and not necessary without—this, too, is a plus in your life.

Humility implies simplicity. See the importance in your life; see the importance in the lives that surround you; see the importance and the significance of the world about you—the world of nature, the world of man. At the same time, know the identity of all these things; some things are temporary and some things are permanent.

Humility implies recognizing kinship, recognizing One-ness, and *becoming* "At-One-With." Many people think of humility as wearing the hair shirt, grovelling, being poor, and so on. True humility is the greatest riches in the whole world. It is the riches of faith, the riches of spirit, the riches of love. It is not poor; it is not feeling pain, poverty, and all these many things. You see, when you truly recognize your One-ness with the Father, you are not poor, *you are the richest person in the world.*

True humility is recognizing one's kinship with all life; not just recognition on the intellectual level, but rather on the intuitive, or nonintellectual, level as well.

Perceiving inwardly?

Yes. If all things have a kinship, and if all things are related and part of One, why do we treat things separately? Why do we divide and say, "these things are good," and "these things are bad"? Separation and kinship are opposed to one another. Kinship means unification. In separating and labeling, things lose their power.

Take the example of a tree: You have a beautiful branch with beautiful leaves, fruit, and flowers; but once you saw that branch off the tree, it dies. You have separated it. This is what man does. He separates himself from the world. True humility is not separation, but unity, blending.

Would you say that true humility is touching the essence of the reality within mankind and being an expression of it?

Yes, unifying with and then expressing it.

You look at a tree and say, "Ah, there is God in the form of a tree. Isn't that wonderful!" And then you look at yourself and say, "Ah, there is God in the form of a man. Isn't that wonderful!" You look all about you, and everything you see is God being expressed in Form. When you realize that surrounding and flowing and permeating all these things is also God (it is not manifested, but it is still existent), you are truly humble.

But if you see all these things and yet behave in a manner

that is in opposition to these truths, you are not humble. Recognition implies a way of life.

There is outward knowing and inward knowing. Both are necessary. The outward knowing we label as "intellect"; the inward knowing we call "intuition"; but they are two forms of the same knowing. One has Form, and the other has not; yet they are one.

I can understand humility as a strength and not as a weakness or as an absence of anything, but how may we convey this to people?

With your life, with your actions. That is the only way. Words, sentences, paragraphs, are only a partial expression. The real expression is living.

Being an example?

Yes, but not necessarily being *an example*. You see, being an example implies, "This is *the way* it is done." Each man is his own example.

Would you care to name some humble people?

Jesus, the Christ, is a good example. Gautama, the Buddha. The one known as Leon. There are many. We find humility on many levels. Some people are totally consumed by it—someone such as Albert Schweitzer. You can drive a Cadillac and still be humble.

12

The Meaning of
Self-Attunement

*Sometime ago you told me to become more physically and
spiritually attuned. What should I do to attain this spiritual
attunement?*

I would suggest first, a daily meditation in the morning or in
the evening. Second, study, so that you can intellectually
unlock the spiritual doors. No study can actually teach you
anything, but studies can provide keys so that you can get to
some of the spiritual treasures that are within you. Then, after
you have studied and become more aware, you can start
working with other people.

*I am presently involved with an Edgar Cayce study group.
Would this be one of the ways of studying?*

This is *an* exposure, yes. It gives you a brief insight into
awareness. I would recommend the study of Yoga and Zen,
the various other philosophers and philosophies. Expand your
consciousness. Do not limit your exposure to this one small
facet.

My husband seems opposed to such studies.

This man is a bit afraid of things of a spiritual nature; he
looks upon them in a rather perverted light. To him they are

crazy and kooky and odd-ball and weird and bear all sorts of labels. Deep down within himself he believes all this, but he is afraid of it. He is afraid to live up to his true potential. If he goes along living as a half-self, with half-awareness, he won't have to take a look at things—so he condemns spiritual studies. But the day will come, not long in the future, when he, too, will become involved.

Can you give me and my family some insight into how to fulfill our missions on Earth?

Each person comes to the earth plane to expand his awareness—his God-awareness, his true self-realization. Anything you expose yourself or your children to that will remind them of their true identity, an identity that is beyond body, beyond time, will help. Do not preach to them or try to give them dogma, but treat them all as if they were bits of the greatest creative force—recognize this within them. Recognize the Christ-consciousness within all these people. They will respond.

How do you achieve awareness?

By recognizing *Who You Are* and *What You Are.* Give credence to it; give power to it. Do not look on what you *are not,* but what you *really are.* You are not just a body. By giving credence to the real, we abandon the false, and thus achieve awareness.

Are there any guidelines that you can give me to help my husband and children to become more spiritually aware?

Become so spiritually aware yourself that you are an example to them. If you are full of joy, peace, tranquility, and harmony, they will notice; and they will want what you have— then you can help them gain. But first you must have spiritual awareness yourself. This is the job ahead: To fill one's own spiritual reservoir, so that it is overflowing and shared by others.

Have you any other suggestions?

You tend to be running around in circles; you need to sit down and be still. You need to look about you, to examine the physical world and to go within yourself and examine what you see there. You are so concerned with outside things and your many activities that you don't have time to examine the things that are real and genuine. Just be still and know.

Love all those who are about you. Don't make demands on them, but give your love freely. Love them for what they are, the way they are, and the life about you, and you will be truly happy within. Let go of this confusion of some of your images of people.

People are not always what you think they are. Try to see the Christ Light in all the people with whom you come in contact. Try to see their perfection, their real persons. In so doing, they and you grow and accomplish something.

You will never accomplish anything by examining all the negative patterns. Examine all the good things you can about them, and emphasize them. Then life about you will become very harmonious and exciting and stimulating—and there will be love far, far beyond that which you now know.

Look in the mirror every morning, but not at the body. Look into the eyes of your soul and know that the living God dwells there within you—and within all the things and people you meet. In this way you will touch many lives.

13

Visualization

What is the difference between perception and conception?
That which you can perceive, you can conceive. And that
which you can conceive, if you believe, you can achieve.

Perception is in the realm of intuition. Conception, on the
other hand, is in the realm of intellect.

When you conceptualize something, it takes on form and
dimension. Perception is usually without form; you perceive
on the abstract level. Then, as you believe, you give this thing
life—you give it power, animation.

And achievement?
Achievement is really just the final touch. The other steps
are far more important, far more exciting. This is the thing
you need to go over, ten thousand-thousand times. Unless this
process becomes automatic, there are voids in life. The unsuc-
cessful person usually leaves one step out, and this is just like
taking a rung out of a ladder—it breaks the rhythm, the
pattern, and things fall through.

How does this relate to visualization?
You can bring that which is real into your reality by

visualizing the real. That which you can visualize you can put into motion and bring into your reality.

This is the difference between the great person and the little man who never goes anywhere. The great man visualizes many things in reality and puts them into motion, thereby bringing them into his reality. He visualizes them as they are in reality, and they become a part of him. This is the method used by great inventors, scientists, and those who do!

What are the steps in visualization?

Practice the following exercise until you can do as directed, easily. Sit down, close your eyes, visualize the following, and feel!

Visualize, concentrate on a rose, intensely, smell the fragrance.

Visualize, concentrate on a fire, strongly, feel the flames, *see* it!

Visualize, concentrate on a warm room, feel the warmth.

Visualize, concentrate on a cold room, feel the cold.

What is the relation between visualization and feeling?

Visualization must be coupled with *feeling* to have it borne into your reality. Visualization is the picture, the tuning-in process. Feeling is the vehicle to bring that which is visualized in reality into *your* reality. Visualization is the *abstract,* and feeling is the *concrete.*

You must visualize, then feel, then experience, like the artist who visualizes the picture, feels the picture, then experiences the picture by painting it. If the chain is broken, if there is neither the feeling nor the visualization, then there cannot be the picture.

You cannot experience unless you visualize, then feel. These are *the magic keys.* If you can truly visualize yourself as a child of God, as perfect, then you are. Visualization goes beyond the thought realm. It is a tuning-in to bring that which is real into your reality.

14

Astral Travel

Many people have asked Louis, "What is astral travel?"

Astral travel is referred to by many labels. It has been called "soul travel," which is a misnomer, because in essence it is not. It has been called bi-location, which is perhaps a little better, more definitive. Even the phrase "astral travel" is not an exact label. I like the term "out-of-the-body experience" myself, because I think it gives it more latitude. For aeons, it seems that man has been leaving his body for many reasons—perhaps out of discontent, perhaps for purposes of study and visiting other dimensions. There are many recorded evidences of this in the Bible and all the writings of the great sages and prophets of old.

Just exactly what takes place?

When one talks about this, one must get rather personal, because it is a personal experience.

I lie down, although I don't think that one would actually have to. I think any relaxed state would be all right. Then it is a matter of willing yourself, of mentally conditioning yourself. You tell yourself, "I am going to be leaving the body, and I want to do thus and so." You should have some motivation, some reason for going; I think the greater the motivation, the easier it is to achieve this thing. I would not advise anyone to try to leave the body just for kicks, because it is not a thing that one does lightly.

Lie down, relax, close your eyes. The process is very similar to going to sleep. You have willed your invisible body to leave your physical body.

What is that like?

The sensation is rather interesting; the nearest I can describe it is that it is like taking your hand out of a rubber glove after you have been washing dishes. Your body feels like a very thin, yet at the same time, heavy rubber glove; and you can almost feel the sensation as you leave the body.

I have been told that it is wise to leave by the head.

I have tried leaving the body at various other points, and have had rather unpleasant sensations. For example, you can leave through the lower extremities of the body. You get a very confused vibration as you pull through this force field. It is not a pleasant experience. You can leave through the solar plexus region. Here the sensation is very much like being on a merry-go-round; it is a very difficult way.

If you leave through the top of the head (the crown chakra), which is the area of higher consciousness or vibratory state, it seems to be much easier. It is as if you are pouring out very gradually, although the whole process takes only a few seconds. In many instances you find yourself suddenly floating over your body and looking down. I remember this happening to me when I was a child.

You are quite aware that you are you and where you are— yet you are quite aware that you are also you, "down there." The experience gives a different awareness of who you really are. If anything could convince you that you are not your body, this does.

You look down and see the body; then you find that the activator, or motivator, that propels this invisible you is caught. As soon as you think a thing, it is so.

Ordinarily, we are very concerned with taking steps and doing this and that. We find ourselves in a rather limited world; we are limited by how fast we can walk, how fast we can do things, and there are certain restrictions put on our activities. Suddenly you find yourself in an unrestricted world where there is no day or night, where there is an unlimited uniforce—unlimited, unhampered; and the physical world is no longer one of the boundaries. Many people find themselves "going to school" when they leave the body. I have had this experience many times.

Could you describe this?

It appears to be a round place, a circular room, shall we say. There do not seem to be any walls, and yet there is something there which appears to be very iridescent—like mother-of-pearl with changing colors. On these occasions, you usually leave the body within just a matter of a split second; you come popping up through the floor, and you find yourself in this place.

You find yourself sitting in a large circle. You and the others there are robed in loose-fitting garments. There are many people in this circle. Shortly, a person appears who gives a lesson or lecture. It is usually something very profound and with great meaning. In my own instances, it has generally dealt with something that I have need of in my life at that time. Many other people have had similar experiences.

I have also found myself visiting friends when I leave the body. In some instances they remember, in some they don't—it depends upon how perceptive that individual is.

What is the purpose of this astral travel?

I think the purpose of out-of-the-body experiences, as of all life, is to grow, to expand, and to teach awareness. I don't think it has much point if you do it for frivolous purposes, but I think you can use it to enter into other realms, other planes of consciousness, and to study.

I have read accounts of people who were incarcerated escaping from their situations by this means.

There have been many instances of people who were in jail and very unhappy about their situations who fled in this fashion. Madame Blavatsky, for example, got much of her information for her Theosophical books, it is said, from certain volumes which were in a secret section of the Vatican

Library. These books were unavailable to her in her mortal form, so she put the mortal form aside, went and did her research, brought back what she wanted, and used it in her writings.

Do you usually re-enter the body at the same point you left?

Yes. My one thought on being about to return used to be: "My God, I have to come back to this heavy body." You feel a great weight; the body seems so heavy and coarse and made of lead; whereas your invisible body has no weight or substance—a very euphoric state.

Some people think that astral traveling is actually meditation; that the goal of meditation is to leave the body.

No, meditation and astral travel are two distinct and separate things. Meditation is basically going within, whereas astral travel is going with-out. Of course, it depends on how one uses the universe; and if you get to the point where there are no such things as within or with-out, you have a different problem, as far as your references are concerned.

You mentioned a loose-fitting robe; do you usually wear clothes when you are astral-traveling?

Yes, usually there appears to be a garment of sorts on the body, though there doesn't seem to be any weight to it.

Are you aware of sex or male and female?

Yes, you are aware of male and female, but not to the degree that we are aware of it on our ordinary mortal plane of endeavor. It doesn't seem to be as pronounced, and yet it does seem to be there.

Are you aware of time?

No, time seems to be laid aside, and there is no such thing as space at that particular moment.

You just will yourself to go somewhere, and you are there?

You are there immediately.

Many people talk about the "silver cord" linking you to the physical body.

Yes, you are always aware of an attachment with the body and that there *is* a body asleep "down there" or someplace.

If something were to happen to the physical body when

one's consciousness were in the astral state, would the cord be severed—if the body were to be burnt in a fire or suffer a heart attack, for instance?

This is what happens at the moment called death—a separation of the invisible part of you from the visible or manifested part.

Also, if you are out of the body and someone shakes you or calls to you very loudly, you find yourself coming back into the body very suddenly. Many people who have had such experiences recall waking up in the morning with a great spastic jerk, almost jumping. This occurs when one has just come back into the body, and it is the muscle reaction to this experience.

You say you feel no mass; nothing has weight.

Nothing has weight, but you are aware of the molecular structure of things. For example, if you are out of the body and you walk through a couch, you are aware of its molecular structure. You are not aware of its weight or density, but you are aware of the fact that it does exist.

You mentioned that you are not aware of day or night. Does there seem to be a light, and if so, where does it come from? What kind of light is it?

The "air" (or surrounding medium) seems to be filled with light; there doesn't seem to be any day or night.

Are you aware of electric lights?

You are aware of everything you are aware of in your ordinary manifested state; but there do not seem to be the same limitations as far as day and night are concerned. For example, you wouldn't ordinarily walk down a dark alley during the nighttime, because you might stumble over something; out-of-the-body you don't have that sensation of night or darkness as a limiting factor.

I heard you mention that you have been able to move a bell.

One thing that is sometimes very frustrating when you are out of the body and in a nonphysical state is that the same laws that apply to your physical state don't apply to your nonphysical state. Consequently, you are not able to pick things up as you do now; your hand goes right through them. I

85

was trying to contact some friends and asked them to put a bell up to see whether I could ring it. They put a bell up over their bed, and my hand just passed through it. Finally they got a very tiny bell, such as is used on key chains, and I found I could cause a molecular action that would ring the bell. I couldn't ring it in the ordinary sense, but I could cause it to ring by a thought process and could contact people that way.

About how often do you do this travel?

Consciously, about once or twice a week. I find myself doing it at other times in an unconscious state; I just find myself out-of-the-body.

Some people consider the experiences of astral travel as a status-giving accomplishment.

The only status that I think a person can achieve is how much he can give. If you are a giving person, you have a right to feel good about it. I don't think astral travel is a status thing. I don't think it is something that should be taken lightly or should be bandied about and played with. It is a real thing and a very serious thing.

The Source was later asked about possible evil influences or evil entities entering a body when a person is traveling astrally or is out of the body.

If all is God, can there be else? Let us not concern ourselves with evil and thus have a two-edged sword. The way is narrow; the way is One, not Two. Man has been so concerned with good and bad, black and white, that he is very confused. Let us focus upon the Good, the Right, the True, the Real. Cast aside all these other shadows. They do not exist unless we want them to. If we want evil, we can have evil. If we want bad, we can have bad. But why would we want them?

15

*R*egeneration
and Rejuvenation

The Father-Mother God is not a person or figure, but is rather
a principle representing the unmanifested and the manifested.
The Father represents that which is unmanifested, and the
Mother represents that which is manifested. Combined, they
represent the *total God.*

In order for anything to exist in a manifested form, it must
first exist on the unmanifested plane; so it is with regeneration
and rejuvenation. Regeneration is the Father Principle—the
unmanifested—and it supplies the energy to generate that
which is necessary for rejuvenation. Regeneration is the power
force behind renewing, and rejuvenation is the process of
making young again. Rejuvenation, then, is the manifested.

You can regenerate and rejuvenate by changing or restructuring the thought process, and by changing actions through
proper exercise and proper breathing. Through proper diet and
breath, you can recirculate and regenerate the life current.

Breathing is too often taken for granted and is commonly a
topic of ignorant speculation. The air you breathe is not
simply a gas to fill your lungs because it is needed to sustain
life—it is a food. The air you breathe contains every mineral

and every vitamin—it is *prana,* the breath of God. Although there are many techniques and different methods of breathing, there is one form that stands out from all the rest. Although all forms of breathing are beneficial, the "life-breathing" technique is the most useful for the average individual.

Rejuvenation-breath is the lifegiving breath. It is more important to you than anything in your life. You can live for ninety days without taking food into your body, but without air, you cannot live more than two and one-half minutes.

The following technique is one of the most beneficial methods of breathing: Feel your own pulse with your finger: (Do not feel the pulse with your thumb for it has a pulse of its own and you will get a "double count.") Inhale through the nostrils to the pulse beat of seven and exhale to the same pulse beat. Seven is the number that is used here, because it has been found that seven beats is a normal length of time for a breath. It has no esoteric meaning.

This is a good rejuvenation-breath exercise, for it relaxes you and makes your body function with a rhythmic pattern. Practice this consciously and it will become a part of your subconscious. Make this rhythmic breathing a part of yourself; it will do you no good unless it becomes a part of your subconscious awareness. Even though you know how to breathe, realize what you're breathing, and also how you are breathing. Breathe with rhythm. *Be aware.*

In each breath you inhale, you absorb some electrons; they act as food and provide energy for your body. In a tension situation, certain inner centers function in reverse and secrete a poison that prohibits the entrance of these electrons. This poison must be overcome, eliminated, or extracted from the body. The above breathing technique is a rapid solution for overcoming this poison. It relaxes your physical body and allows it to feed properly on the air consumed—proper nourishment thus occurs.

Also, this breathing technique, when coupled with positive thinking and correct thought placement, will help you develop your intuition.

Positive, well-directed thought in a relaxed or harmonious

atmosphere is necessary for the development of your inward forces, your intuition.

Color is another important factor in the process of rejuvenation and can be used as a supplement in your breathing routine. Make a conscious effort three or four times a day to concentrate on the seven basic colors (red, orange, yellow, green, blue, indigo, violet) as you inhale. You need do this for only a minute or so for the cells in your body to benefit. As you inhale, visualize one color with each pulse beat. Actually see and feel the color.

Notice the colors that people wear and how they act on a certain day wearing a specific color. If you recall the wearing apparel of someone close to you, you will find that his or her "mood" is related to the color directly surrounding him, usually his clothes. A person's general attitude can be predicted from the color of the clothing he wears and the color with which he generally associates or surrounds himself. Notice your own reaction to color. What was your basic wearing color two days ago, and what was your mood? What is your basic clothing color today, and what is your mood?

As we mentioned earlier, air is *prana;* but so is water, another very important factor in the rejuvenation of the self. The best water for you is water that is fresh, alive, vibrant, and pure. The same is true of foods.

Spring water is live water, as contrasted with distilled water, which is dead. The body requires live food for nourishment, not dead or decayed foods. (Distilled water, canned vegetables and juices, and so on, are all dead foods.) Dead foods merely fill the body and stuff it; they do not nourish it properly.

Water should *never* be taken with a meal, but may be taken before and after eating. A minimum of eight glasses of water—spring water, if possible—is recommended daily. Chlorinated or treated water may harm the system and should never be consumed unless it is the only water available. If the water in your area is not alive and vibrant, we recommend that you purchase spring water for drinking. The expense incurred in the purchase of bottled water is minimal, and good water is very important for the regeneration and rejuvenation process.

The following procedure will enable you to charge, or make vibrant, the water you use for drinking: Place water in a pure copper vessel and let it stand for eight hours or more. Copper is a good conductor and will charge and energize the water. If you do not have a copper vessel, try this method: Place plain spring water in a real crystal (not glass) container. (The better the crystal, the better the results.) For at least an eight-hour period; cover the crystal container of water with a silk or fine linen cloth. This will help purify the water and enhance its pristine form.

Food, of course, is also necessary for the regeneration and rejuvenation process, and the proper foods for consumption are those which are alive. For those who are vegetarians and also for those who are nonvegetarian, the following combination is a powerful protein supplement that should be consumed daily.

FOREVER YOUNG FOOD

Mix together in a blender:

2 cups peanut butter	1 cup crushed sunflower seeds
2 cups raw honey	1 cup crushed coconut
1 cup wheat germ oil	1 cup toasted sesame seeds
1 cup crushed or ground almonds	1 cup chia
	1 cup lemon juice

The above combination was given by the Source, and it was stated that this is very high in protein, that one tablespoonful is equal to one cup of meat. This is a complete regeneration protein food.

The physical, mental, and spiritual bodies cannot be separated; as we strive to rejuvenate and regenerate one, we must also strive to rejuvenate and regenerate all three. Meditation and study, if acted upon, help to accomplish this with our spiritual and mental bodies. The above food suggestions help to accomplish this with our physical selves. You must *do;* you must *act;* you must *develop all three bodies simultaneously.*

16

The Education and Guidance of Youth

Many parents have asked Louis how they can best help their children.

Be an example; be that which you want your children to be.

If you would have them be honest, then be honest in all things.

If you would have them be of good cheer, be of good cheer yourselves.

If you want them to be loving, then you, too, must be loving.

Show them a pattern, and they will follow it. Teach them that they, too, are filled with this thing called God, this magnificence, this perfection, this Perfection beyond perfection, this Light of all lights. And teach them that they are very important.

Teach them that they will walk in darkness, yet there will always be light; that there will be error about them in their world, yet behind this error there is purpose.

Teach them that all things are of God, and in their essence, pure. If you perceive God, if you know God, then God is in your life. This is the greatest gift that you can give your children.

What is the parents' obligation regarding the education of their children?

To expose their children to all the many facets of life, to show them many things; but most of all, to be an example. If you want your children to be Shining Lights in the world, to be kind, good, honest, and true, and have all the other virtues you consider necessary, then you must be that yourselves. How can you cheat on your income tax and tell your children to be honest?

Parenthood is a divine obligation. Children are not *ours;* they are God's, and only in our care. While they are in our care we have an obligation not to yell at them or shame them or scold them, but to be examples toward which they can mold themselves.

We have few *parents* today. We have many seed planters and incubators, but it seems to stop there. Many like to plant seeds, and some get stuck with the job of incubating, but it often ends there. Consequently, these by-products of man's pleasures go into the world.

What is the relation between education and schools?

The learning process, the thing called education, is an area that is highly esteemed by mankind, yet one with many discrepancies, many voids, many treadmills.

A school must be a continuing thing. The role of the instructor, teacher, or guidance director is to see that there is a pattern, a continuum, a sequence. This is how you learn—by sequences. One thing leads to another, and so on. This is a structuring process, and more intuitive than you might realize. Learning is a bringing forth of that which has already been learned, and applying it to your present life form.

What about lessons, then?

The function of lessons is to trigger off within each student an awareness he already has. We do not *teach* people anything; they already *know* it. All we do is take off some caps, as you might uncap a well under pressure, and let the precious substance spew forth.

What does the teacher do, then?

The role of an educator is to excite, to stimulate, to provide an environment where these things can take place; this is done in many ways. It should be fun; it should be exciting; it should be stimulating. If it is boring, dull, and unexciting, it creates gaps so that the flow cannot get through. Unfortunately, too much of this is done in the name of "education."

Give the child a challenge that will stimulate what he already knows, then what is inside will come through to meet that challenge.

What is thinking?

Thinking is a receptive process, basically intuitive. As we have said many times, "Man *thinks* that he thinks, and yet he is not capable of thinking." Man *is* capable of receptivity.

With the young person, it is good to introduce a pattern of exposure both to words and to quietness, stillness. In colleges or universities, there is too much stress on the word. There should be more emphasis on what lies *behind* the word. How can you understand a word if you do not comprehend what lies behind it? You must always strive to balance any situation.

Thinking is receptivity; making yourself a channel, freeing yourself from things like prejudice, fear, doubt, hatred. In letting go of these things, the human being becomes a receptive channel, and this thing we label *thinking* can take place.

From a metaphysical point of view, human beings tend to think in terms of structures, relating one structure to another. Thinking forms the bridges between the structures and creates unified patterns; but if we are to go beyond this pattern into the abstract, into the void, then we can comprehend more totally.

What should a learning center be?

It should be a place of peace—not the peace that is pictured as a dove flying, but peace that comes from cooperation, from understanding, from appreciation, and from mankind fulfilling its destiny.

A learning center can be the hub of a large wheel, with the spokes going out in many directions and encompassing the planet. Roads go from and come to such a place. From here, young people can go into many cultural patterns, and many can be brought to this place from other peoples.

What are the basics to be learned at such a center?

First of all, the students should be able to read. Perhaps only forty to fifty percent of students going into colleges know how to read—by reading, we mean not just viewing words, but comprehension of ideas, feelings, emotions, patterns. Reading gives the student a platform, a foundation, a background.

Secondly, communication, which has many ramifications. A student should learn that we communicate verbally (which is a very inadequate form of communication), and through our bodies, our minds, and our actions. If man is to progress toward understanding, toward brotherhood, he must be able to communicate. Once you understand another individual, once you can meet upon common ground, then you can make progress working together. As long as you have barriers between you, little can be accomplished.

How do you teach this communication?

In this learning and communication center, the languages of the world should be taught—not the languages of yesterday, but the languages of today. Here we would also find art, music, and dance, which are nonverbal forms of communication.

Can you suggest an approach to the study of foreign languages which will result in maximum effectiveness in personal communication in the shortest possible time?

First of all, we object to the word "foreign," because this implies "apart from." Let us just say "languages."

We would suggest that the student be completely submerged in a language pattern. If a student can relate to that language on many levels, he can comprehend it better. If he can enter into the vibration from which the language was given birth and allow his own vibrational force field to be unified with that of the language, he can understand it more easily.

Language should not be a dead, uninteresting subject, but a vital, exciting thing. So often "educators," in their smugness, try to limit a language to books. How can you do this? It is stupid. Language cannot be limited to the written page. Every language has its verbal and nonverbal aspects, and both are equally important. Languages can best be learned by the student being submerged in them, being a part of them. It should be not just one hour of his daily regime, but an around-the-clock part of his pattern. Then he truly learns.

Learning is a total thing, not segmented. This is the big fallacy, the big fraud in education today. Learning has been cut up, dissected, segmented. Learning is a whole, not a part; when you teach from the whole, there arises understanding, knowledge. When you teach from the part, you get merely "knowing *about*," and it has little value.

Should language study be a requirement for all students in a learning center?

In the world today we can no longer look upon ourselves as an isolated island. We must start thinking not of *a* country, *a* language, but of countries and of languages. Therefore, if a student is truly educated, he must be exposed to many languages and cultural patterns.

Should cultural differences be identified and protected, insofar as possible?

In essence, there is only one culture: mankind. Man has many different ways of expressing himself; you might label these as "cultural differences."

It would be better to study cultural *patterns* and consider the similarities, rather than the differences. There is far more unification in cultural patterns than the average person might think. There are different names and approaches, but basically, all mankind has the same needs.

It is good to enter into the vibrational pattern of another group of persons because, as we do, we take on new understanding.

But do not look at the differences, for these are walls, and we must not be concerned with walls. Look instead to the similarities, to the linking and unifying factors. These are important.

Is there a role that colleges or other learning centers can play in the development of these similarities?

A college or learning center should be a place of exposure—correct exposure. So often we look at other cultural patterns

95

like the small child going to the zoo, who says, "Oh, look at the animal in the cage! Isn't he different?" This is not the approach to understanding of a vital educational center. We must take away the cages; we must work side by side, in partnership.

It would be well for college students, for example, to eat the food that is eaten in other places, to be exposed to the media of other places, and most important, not to look upon any of these things as dissimilar, but to see the similarities. Too much stress has been placed upon differences; differences are not important. The important things that we can teach are the similarities. This approach unifies.

We must do away with the concepts, motivations, and approaches that tend to segment things. We must look to that which unifies—music, for example; art, dance. These unifying media are the things we must explore, feel, become a part of. It is very difficult to understand anything if you merely read about it or talk about it. You need to *experience* things.

A college or university should be an experience center; a place where people can experience things, not on a phoney level, but on a real, genuine one.

It is the young who will open the doors. It is the young who will tread the highways, coming and going. It is the young who will reach out their hands. Unfortunately, many of today's older generations are caught up in patterns of smugness, of selfishness, and they do not care to share.

But the new generation, today's young, have a completely new viewpoint. Many are the Christians and Buddhists of old, and by combining these two thought patterns—that of love and that of wisdom—tremendous things take place. Love provides the strength, wisdom provides the tools; together they produce peace—not a peace that is static, but a peace that is alive and vibrant, flowing and producing. And from this peace comes joy.

17

On Seeing Auras

Louis: Auras depend on how people are psychically constructed.

A person who has a chip on his shoulder, gets mad, and releases the whole thing, will have reds coming out in his aura.

If you are looking at an aura, you will often see different shades of red, all the way from pink to crimson.

Pink we call the color of love; it is a pearly, iridescent pink. When a person loves someone or is loved by someone, when a parent loves a baby, you will find this pink coming out.

If a person gets angry with you, you will notice red spots shooting out; or if he gets terribly excited about something, the aura might have some red showing through the eyes.

Another color you might see is a deep orange. Of course, there are thousands of shades of orange; but if you see the Halloween orange with a metallic look to it in a person, you know this is the kind of person who really gets things done. This color may also indicate a healthy appetite; such a person likes his food. The exact interpretation depends on the amount of color you see, of course.

You might see yellow in a person's aura; this is a sharp

character, the fellow who gets the "A's" in school. Look around a classroom sometime if you are tuned in, and you'll see this yellow around some of the people. Or observe a bunch of kids together taking an exam and you will see a lot of yellow shooting out, because they are really concentrating. When somebody is trying to make out his income tax forms or is really thinking hard, his aura will be yellow.

You might see green around a person, although again, there are many shades of green. If you see a dirty, muddy green, you know that person is greedy; he is going to grab money or anything he can. He wants to put it in his pocket and is not too much in favor of passing any of it along. If you see that ugly green around a person, don't have too much to do with him; be polite to him and let him go his way.

But a pure green, a nice, light, forest green comes from a person who is pretty well-balanced; he doesn't go overboard on anything, but stays in the middle of the road.

You might see a blue. The blue that you see in auras is produced when people are inspired. They might be inspired by a number of different things: They might see a pretty painting or they might look at the scenery. Many things can inspire and lift them up and make them feel a bit taller than they are. If you are very happy—if, say, you helped somebody do something and you feel really good inside—this blue will come. People such as nurses, who try to help others, will show this blue shooting out.

The color which we call indigo is very hard to describe: a violet with blue in it, a bluish light; you see it occasionally. This indicates a psychic or sensitive or intuitive person, a person who feels things not so much with his eyes and ears, but senses them intuitively.

Violet indicates a type of dedication to a nonbusiness world; such a person is more involved in another world than a materialistic one.

You will find variations of these colors and you may see them change. For example, people walking into church might be thinking, "When am I going to hear about my income tax?" or things of that sort. Watch what happens in church, what really turns them on. Instead of being inspired, they are thinking, "How am I going to make $75?" You *should* see in a church quite a marvelous variety of blues and purples and violets, but they are not always there; other colors may come shooting out.

Gray could be an indication of many things. Physical ailments could show up with gray, and mentally ill people usually have grays.

Usually with physical ailments it is a yellowish gray, whereas mental illness has a bluish, or sometimes a purplish tint. If you find just a little bit of gray, the subject may be a little bit ill—a headache or stomachache. If you find a lot of gray in a person's aura, it might be an indication that he is about to leave the body, to die.

Brown indicates doubts—questioning, doubting. If a person can't think something out, he might have a lot of brown in his aura. If you are working as a psychic, for example, and you see brown, you know that your subjects think you are full of cheese—and that is fine; *you* know that you are not full of cheese and it doesn't matter.

Sometimes you see gaps in an aura. Sometimes an aura will shoot out in one place and be smaller in other places. I don't think there is any true black in auras.

Occasionally you will see very large auras, although these big ones are rare. People's auras usually jump out when they are in a highly emotional state, such as when they get very excited or they are much in love or inspired.

When people meditate, their auras change. When they eat, their auras change. Everything you do affects your aura. The colors you find around people change constantly.

When you can't get along with somebody—you don't know why, but you just don't like him—I have found that usually, when I have been able to analyze the situation, it is an auric clash. For example, if a person who is very love-oriented comes into contact with someone who is very intellectual and has no room in his life for love, for whom everything has to be black and white and in a little box or he can't accept it, there is bound to be a clash between the two.

You can also observe one aura feed off another. If a very inspirational person or a person with high confidence walks into a room and mingles with people, he will affect the auras of others. Their auras will begin to take on his color. That is why you should be very careful with whom you associate, because you become part of a person as you associate with him.

Smoking tends to produce a deadening effect on the aura; it drains the life force out of it.

Some drugs do weird things to auras. I have watched the auras of people who are tripping, shoot here and there in strange patterns.

We don't know one one-thousandth of the effects of drugs on people. With repeated use, marijuana starts producing a lethargic pattern; you can observe the change in the aura. Someone very alert and bright and sparkly, who gets hooked on marijuana for six weeks or so, develops a very lifeless, listless aura. Drugs definitely do affect the life-force. Even aspirin affects it.

Various rooms affect people's auras. If you walk from one room into another, your aura changes. It is most fascinating to watch.

When I was in Rome, I watched people go into the cathedrals and the museums to see all the beautiful paintings. I watched their auras start brightening up as they started looking.

Being out in nature affects people's auras—they brighten and get bigger. Cities don't do very good things for auric patterns. Auras there are usually very confined, and you don't find many shooting out, or very happy and vibrant auras.

18

Color and Its Uses

When we speak of color, we speak on many levels, and it is this many-dimensional aspect that gives rise to misunderstandings and confusion.

Pigmented color comes from the earth and is the color the artist uses on the canvas. This is the color most used in our everyday world, from clothing dye to housepaint.

Prismatic color is produced as light passes through a prism; it is similar to a rainbow.

The auric, or cosmic, dimension of color has been witnessed by only a few, and those who have been privileged to view it are very aware of a whole new dimension of color. This color is alive and vibrant; whereas the other dimensions, comparatively speaking, are drab and dead. Cosmic color represents spiritual manifestation; pigmented color represents material manifestation; and prismatic color represents scientific manifestation.

In the cosmic realm, as in other realms, there are seven basic colors, but please do not think that these are all the colors. As you grasp insight into their representation, do not fall into the trap of thinking that you comprehend all there is to know about them. They are very complicated, and as with other dimensions, there are thousands and thousands of shades, blends, and so forth. For simplicity's sake, however, we shall take the liberty of placing three-dimensional labels on seven basic para-dimensional colors.

As we enter the higher or spiritual realms, there are no labels, no shackles, such as those as found in the three-dimensional world; so we are labeling colors that have no labels with words that are meant for pigmented or prismatic colors. But until the day comes that each of us shall see these and understand these with the unspoken word and awareness, we are forced to communicate with verbal, three-dimensional language.

Let us discuss Auric or Cosmic Color, remembering that we will be comprehending it with the intellect, rather than with the intuitive from which it springs.

Red: This color is most often referred to as the power-house. It is also known as the color of the harlot and the color of the Christ, for during his ministry on earth, Jesus wore the red, or scarlet robe as he proceeded with his healing work. It is also the color of the body (man) and stands for the five-pointed star.

Red is also the color of beginning, the color of essence, and from this man spirals upward—just as the five-pointed star goes in many directions, so also can man.

As you look into some of the most holy places on earth, or what is thought to be the most holy—again, it is a matter of labels—you will find great quantities of red. The great cathedrals, St. Peter's, the Vatican, show a predominance of red in their stained-glass windows, the color of the Christ, the color of man.

Orange: This is an interesting color in that it represents activity, action. Show me a person who has great quantities of orange in his aura, and I'll show you a person who gets things done. These people are directed with a purpose or with a commitment, not simply running around in circles. This is the color of the hard worker, the active one—not necessarily spiritual activity, but more often activity on the physical plane.

Yellow: This is the color of intellect and should not be confused with its counterpart in another dimension, intuition, for there is a vast difference between the two. You can find intellect contained in books, but you will never find wisdom contained therein. Wisdom is found in the unwritten form.

Yellow is the color of the mathematician and the color of the problem-solver, the scientists working on the space program. Most people will have a great deal of yellow in their aura when they are working or concentrating on a problem; and then, as they pursue something else of a less intense nature, the yellow slowly fades.

Green: Green has interesting ramifications and is the color of exchange, barter, balance. All exchanges should be a balancing. All persons entering into a business dealing should benefit, and the end result should be a balanced situation, not a maneuvering for one-upmanship. On the spiritual level, business should be a balanced exchange.

Not only does green appear in the monies of the world in predominance, but it also is in the color of nature. Here it acts as a balancer to consume the carbon dioxide and give forth oxygen. It provides life through exchange and balance.

Green is also the pivotal point, or fulcrum, between red, orange, and yellow on the one hand; and blue, indigo, and violet on the other. The first three represent the manifested or Mother Principle, while the latter represent the unmanifested or Father Principle.

Blue: This color may be referred to as being the gateway to awareness, to spirituality, to true understanding. It represents the level of man's growth of becoming less and less involved and concerned with things of the flesh and body. It represents man as he reaches a point in his search where he is ready for the deep probing, where he realizes that wisdom is not to be found in books and is not a part of this world.

Indigo: Strange, because it is seldom found in nature, indigo is the color of intuition and represents *knowing* rather than knowing *about*. Knowing comes from universal awareness and is something to strive for, and yet it dwells within us all—we all have the keys.

Violet: This is closely related to the color of the Christ; but here the unmanifested aspect is represented, whereas the red represents the manifested Christ, the man. This is the Christ Consciousness, the potential within us all—the perfection for which we strive. It can be referred to as the violet flame. It is the color of Cosmic Consciousness on its highest level.

Black and White: Black is the absence of color, and white represents all colors. Black represents the unmanifested, and white the manifested. Neither is actually a color.

You will hear many interpretations of color by many persons, and as you do, try to determine on what level they are speaking and their understanding of that level. All the colors on any level are related, just as the notes on a scale are related to the notes on another scale. They may seem different, especially as related to their proximity, but the laws of the universe that pertain to one pertain to the others.

Remember once again, the colors discussed here are the colors of the intangible spiritual realm and cannot be fully comprehended by the intellect. These colors go beyond intellect, beyond this dimension, beyond words. As intuition is of another realm, these colors, too, must be comprehended on another level.

Louis

The front of the Outlook Inn on Orcas Island, home of the Louis Foundation

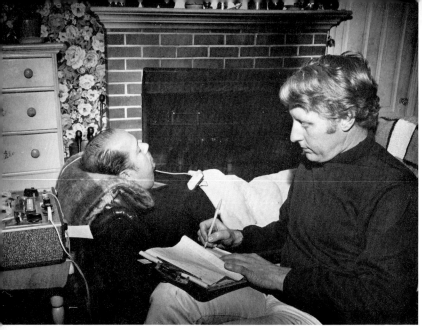

Louis' consultation/meditation/trance room. Starr Farish is always present during Louis' deep meditative trance

The same room, photographed without a flashbulb. Note the energy force field apparently connecting with Louis' solar plexus. The photographer insists his negative is clean and that there was no error in the developing process

The St. Francis Grotto, adjoining Outlook Inn

A typical evening gathering of the Foundation
in the Outlook Inn dining room

Ongoing work at the Foundation: adding rooms to Outlook Inn

Louis looking out over Orcas Island's fishing bay

19

Reincarnation

Lucille Powers said of Louis: "He helps in many ways. One morning he called me long distance. 'Go see Clara,' he said. 'Let her know she has some friends.'

"Clara is one of our study group. She had no phone. The import of the mystifying message escaped me at the time, but as I had a houseful of company, I called another member, Hope, and asked her to go. Later, Hope reported back to me, 'Clara is fine.' But the next morning Clara's husband committed suicide.

"I called Louis. 'I know,' he said sadly."

To the same lady, Louis said, "Each of us, as a spirit desiring to return to this world, is anxious to work out his Karma. The incarnating entity deliberately chooses the parents whom he feels will supply the basic situation necessary for him to learn whatever it is he has to learn. Think. Meditate on this, until you discover the thing you had to learn, the thing your parents forced you to learn, because of their very circumstances."

Asked for further comments on Karma, Louis continued:

It has been written, "As a man soweth, so he shall reap." In essence, this is what Karma is. As we go along in this process we call life and living, we constantly place the things that occur in a great cosmic bank account; all is being recorded constantly.

As we plant certain seeds in our garden, we have a certain harvest. There is a Divine justice, and every man lives under it. We may complain of fortune; but nevertheless, there are no accidents, there are no mislaid things, no lost things. It is all part of a great pattern. This pattern we have put into effect by our actions, by our thoughts, by everything that we do.

How can one best fulfill his Karmic pattern?

You can either take out of your cosmic bank account, or put into it. The balancing of Karma is giving to life more than you take from it. It is giving—not always measured, because that which you can measure and count out is of the least importance—sharing of yourself.

Here is the Real, here is that which you must share. Be of service; and as you give, you are putting into your Karmic bank account. Give your all, not a part, and you shall fulfill your Karmic pattern.

Is mental retardation some type of Karmic pattern?

Yes, it is Karmic.

Will teaching help in any way, or is retardation a set pattern?

Usually a person comes to the earth plan to participate, to function in the world. The retarded come to absorb what is here, but not to function in, or participate in, the activities in the total sense. Naturally, there is some participation.

Why do they come to observe? Are they young in this world?

Yes. They come to learn, but so do all individuals. Any time that a person thinks that he knows it all, that is the time he should take an inventory. Yet it *is* all there within themselves.

Everyone living on the planet Earth has Karmic patterns to fulfill. We fulfill them by trying to be very loving persons. Love in deed, in thought; love in our every action.

Love can transcend Karma, for love is the grace spoken of in the Bible. Try to be a loving person. *Be* love, *breathe* love; and the Karma will pass away.

106

Can you tell us something about the creation of the soul and its relationship to reincarnation?

As each individual begins his incarnation pattern, there is a place within him, an individualization of God, and this we call soul. As man goes through lifetime to lifetime, this personalization of God goes with him. As man grows and becomes more aware, the soul in turn becomes more aware; because the soul is a reflection of the outer, and the outer is a reflection of the inner.

Many people seem to find things quite complicated in the beginning. Man begins a perfected soul, and the same type of perfected soul goes through many lifetimes.

Is the soul as an entity ever lost?

No, there is no such thing as a lost soul. There are some which are wandering in darkness—they are unaware, but they are not lost. Nothing is ever lost. Misplaced or misdirected, yes, but not lost.

What is the purpose of incarnating over a period of time? Is it to attain an awareness of consciousness?

Yes. You might think of the process as resembling a rose. The first petals open, then the second, then the third. As each petal opens, the rose becomes more beautiful and the perfume becomes stronger. It is so with man, as he goes from lifetime to lifetime—each lifetime represents an opening, a new awareness. You might not understand what is happening with your brother or sister, but it is happening, nevertheless. Sometimes the basis is physical, sometimes spiritual, but each person is growing and expanding; and a new awareness comes with each dawning of a new day.

Is the state of Cosmic Consciousness attained after completing all necessary incarnations simply a formless awareness?

Yes. Man but goes into his true identity.

What effect do past lives play on the present life, and what is the lesson to be learned here?

Every man is a totality. He is comprised of many, many life patterns. They're all rolled up into one. The pattern is complicated, yet simple. Each man has one basic lesson to learn, and that is God-hood—who he is, what he is, and where he is going.

A lady wrote that previous lives were a curiosity to her, and inquired as to the associations at present with individuals whom she had never met before.

I would not call previous lives a curiosity. It seems to be a word associated with something on a very minor level, on a speculative level. Past lives are a reality, not a curiosity.

You [the subject of this reading] have had many past lives, as you know, mostly in the East. This is your home. The people with whom you come into contact in this life pattern are those with whom you have had associations in the past. In many instances you came together to work out, or work through, the Karmic patterns.

For example, you have had many lifetimes with the person to whom you are now married, and none of the life patterns have been resolved harmoniously. In this lifetime you must establish a balanced pattern with this individual so that both of you can grow. But you have had many lifetimes, hundreds upon hundreds, with the people you meet in this life pattern.

What effect should the previous history of my soul have on my present life, personality, work, and so on?

Because your soul permeates your body, there is an influence on all facets of your life. For example, had you been an alcoholic in the last life and lost your life from this excess, it is very likely that in this life you would have a complete distaste for alcohol.

Your soul with all its memories does influence everything in this lifetime. As a totality, you are the sum total of everything you have ever been. Of course, your environmental pattern at present adds its touch; but basically, all your drives and feelings and desires come from past life experiences.

A common question asked is, "What past life experiences

would it help me to know about in this life?" On some occasions, the answer takes this form:

You have enough to do to cope with the present pattern. It would do you little good at this point in your development to glimpse the past. You would be even more confused than you are at the moment. It would be best that you do not lift the veil at this time.

Be concerned with the present, the circumstances about you right now.

However, on many occasions, Louis speaks more freely of past lives and past associations: "Has this group that has gathered together known each other before?"

Yes, there are many cultural patterns represented here. Basically, the people here are from Egypt. This is a gathering of old friends—perhaps new in this lifetime, but in terms of antiquity, no. They know this.

On another occasion:

Yes, this is a gathering together again. You came together basically to love one another, to help one another on a personal basis; and you came together to help mankind on a nonpersonal basis. Each of you has much to contribute, but sometimes you tend to forget who and what you are and just exactly what you are doing. You get caught up in a whirlpool of doubt and confusion.

Louis has, of course, given many individual readings which involve past lives and their relationship to the present one. Four of these will be presented as examples.

I.

Could you tell me more about the Egyptian incarnation you mentioned?

Actually, there were three incarnations in Egypt, two male and one female.

The first was as a boy slave, brought into Egypt by her

conquering armies. His background was of two lines, one in the North and one in the South. This lad took great favor with the captain of the night guards. Since the captain and his wife were childless, he being impotent, he took this child as his son and raised him in the military life. It was a life of being trained to kill others, plunder, take. You left the body in this incarnation at the age of twenty-eight. You left behind you several wives, one of whom was to bear you as her child a few years hence.

In this second lifetime you were born in the female body. Since your mother was an entertainer, a dancer, your life was surrounded by revelry. At a very early age you were raped by one of your mother's drunken admirers. Since your body was not capable of handling such a physical involvement, there was an infection that remained untreated, and you died within a few months.

The next liftime finds you again in Egypt in the hall of Atila, the sculptor, the artisan, during the reign of Ramses. Since you are the only son of this gentleman, you are taught his art. Atila does not know it, but you are not really his son, but that of a servant with whom your mother was having an affair, since Atila is past sixty.

Atila trained you in his art, and you learned well. You find ways that please the members of the court and soon gain favor there. In this lifetime you do much painting, much creative work, and there is even an interest in that which is spiritual and in the concept of God.

Your father leaves the body, and you take over the shop. You take a number of wives and several male lovers as well. Because you are taken with the life of royalty, you find yourself drinking. As you reach your forty-fourth year, you leave the body due to cirrhosis of the liver.

Am I now associating with persons who were formerly friends and acquaintances of mine during the days of my Egyptian reincarnations?

Yes, you have met many; and you will meet others, for this was a very strong, dominant pattern in your life force.

It was your Oriental-Chinese incarnations that most

influenced your present being, for it was in China that you learned to look into the skies and know the mysteries of the stars.

I have studied the Tarot and I feel that I have been closely associated with this kind of thing before.

Yes, the teachings are not new to you. It would be well if you would delve into the various aspects of the Tarot and its different schools and regional representations. This will reveal much to you.

About my elder daughter—can you tell me how I was associated with her before, and possibly what is the cause of her cancerous condition?

You have known her a number of times in another—many other—relationships. This physical condition now present in her body is a Karmic one. Be kind to her, and understanding. Teach her what you know to be true.

For some reason I have had a closer relationship with my younger daughter.

Yes. You came into this lifetime to be the teacher of your elder daughter. With your younger, who is a most joyous soul, there is a very close relationship—at times, more like that of sisters than of mother and daughter. Your role is different with these two individuals. One came in to learn with you as a teacher; the other came to keep you company, to be a kindred spirit.

Can you tell me, have you and I, Louis, been together in other lifetimes?

Yes, our paths have crossed, and they will yet cross again many times in the days ahead.

What is the time of my birth?

You were born just as the sun began to rise and the sound of the bird was heard. You came forth to this earth because you came to give light. Your life is to be that of one who walks in light and spreads the light about where he goes.

Remember always that you are to light many lights. Do not always be unhappy if you do not light bonfires. Be concerned that you do light the light, however small and flickering. You came to give light.

111

II.

Many, many years ago in another body this individual was sacrificed as an offering to the gods. At this time, the person was male and very young. This sacrificial ceremony was thought to bring good things to the people. The body was laid upon an altar, and with a gold, semi-circular knife, it was cut open while the boy was still alive and the entrails were taken out. This person still feels that ceremony, and consequently there are aches and pains in the intestines. For the physical side of this situation, we would recommend that this person take acidophilus culture and a lot of yogurt; drink a great deal of buttermilk, and eat papayas and fresh (not canned) pineapple. We also recommend vitamin C, vitamin B, and iron tablets.

III.

Did I ever do anything worthwhile in any of my former incarnations?

It depends on what you call worthwhile. If you mean were you ever a king, a queen, or a princess, or anyone of royal birth—I see no pattern of that sort. I would say that your pattern up to this point has included some worthwhile lives, yes; but I do not see any glamorous, impressive ones.

By worthwhile, I mean a person of very high spiritual nature—more aware than at present, for instance.

No, nor are you aware of your true self at this time. You're getting there; you're striving and trying to express your real self.

Did I live my past lives in many countries?

Yes, primarily in Egypt, Greece, Turkey, and Mexico. The pattern has been both male and female. You have had many lifetimes involved in music, so in this lifetime there should be an ability or appreciation of music, rhythm, and dancing. When you were young in this lifetime you liked to dance.

Can you explain what I was doing, for instance, in Egypt?

In Egypt you were the wife of a potter. He made clay pots and sold them for cooking and storage vessels.

Did he live in a large city?

Yes, in Thebes, a rather large city. It was during the building of the Great Pyramids.

Did I help with this?

Not directly, no; you were just an observer.

Can you tell me something about my lifetime in Greece?

In Greece you were a maker of stringed musical instruments. You were male, and music was a very paramount thing for you in this life. You prided yourself upon your fine instruments.

And the lifetime in Mexico?

In Mexico you had one lifetime as an Aztec Indian and another as a Mayan Indian. These were both female incarnations. During the Aztec incarnation, you were one of the keepers of the temple. You died from a serpent wound while walking through the forest.

Would you like to say anything about any of my other incarnations?

I would like to talk about this lifetime. You came into this life pattern with a birth that was something of a struggle; your delivery was rather difficult.

You came into a family that found it very difficult to comprehend your dimensionality. But in this lifetime, you will reach forth to new dimensions, new spiritual frontiers.

Cast aside this feeling of inferiority; cast aside your ideas of "little me." Remember that you are a child of God, and as such, a very important person. Although you are but a drop, you are a part of a Great Cosmic Ocean. Do not forget this.

IV.

What exactly was I in my two prior lives? I have a strong feeling that present psychological problems are related to these lives.

In the lifetime just prior to this one, you were a nun in France—although you were not French, but Italian by birth. You joined the order as a very young girl. You were very unhappy with the disciplines, for they were very strict. The things that made you happy did not make for a conventional religious life.

You were most obstinate. You went on a starvation fast to show your opposition to some of the philosophy, and the body was in such a weakened condition that you died of pneumonia. You were about nineteen years old when you died. You had taken the name of Sister Theresa.

As we go to the lifetime prior to this, I see you living in Scotland. You were born into a large family; your father was a farmer and specialized in livestock. As a young girl, you were especially fond of the rabbits and other animals and very close to your father. You married a neighborhood lad when you were very young and innocent. He was about nineteen or twenty and you about sixteen or seventeen. You lived with his family. After you were married about a year and a half, you found yourself with child. In giving birth to the child you lost your life. That is why there are certain fears about giving birth to a child in this lifetime.

Then my present psychological problems are related to my past lives?

Yes; they are related indirectly—some of the fears and some of the doubts. Basically, your problem stems from a deep-seated feeling of inferiority. You do not feel that you are attractive. These fears are unfounded, but they are there, nevertheless.

To a well-known psychic, Louis said:

You have tremendous potential because you have the responsibility of lighting many candles; but you must expand your circle. It is much too small. Yours must be a center of learning, learning in the truer sense, not only astrological; for that is only one slice of the pie. It is time to reach out, the New Age is here, not yesterday, not tomorrow, but now. It is here, and those in the field need to reach out, to expand, to reach more and more people. You feel so inadequate, and you have carried a feeling of inferiority with you for so many years—it is time to throw aside the cocoon and fly.

It is time, and there are no limitations but those which you place upon yourself. You must remember that you have a spiritual obligation. You are not where you are accidentally; you were placed there to do a job. The job is far more expansive, far more comprehensive, than is now being experienced. Open wide the doors, make the light within yourself a burning torch, for that light is needed to reach not a few, but thousands.

You have had many lifetimes lived on this earth plane and on other planets, in other galaxies, but this is *the* lifetime, the important lifetime. You have a mission. You have within your grasp thousands and thousands of keys, and you must see that they are distributed to the multitudes.

20

$\mathcal{M}$emories of Lemuria, a Civilization Before Our Own

Editor's note: The myth of a world before our own has become one of the most persistent of all legends, and echoes of the destruction of a once great civilization seem to be preserved in the folklore of every people. It matters little whether one terms this previous civilization Atlantis, Lemuria, or Mu—or whether one maintains that each of those legendary nations were contemporaneous with one another. Regardless of how one perceives this myth, the question remains of whether there really was a physical Atlantis-Lemuria-Mu, a highly evolved society that colonized the world, charted the surface of the globe, and perhaps even managed to leap into space.

In an earlier work*, I stated that I had come to believe that civilization on Earth has been cyclical and that there have been highly evolved human or hominid cultures before our present epoch. Atlantis-Lemuria-Mu may have become but a symbol of man's racial memory of that time before our own. Within man's collective unconscious may lie half-forgotten memories

---

Mysteries of Time and Space, Prentice-Hall, 1974.

of a time when man-creatures lived in godlike splendor while emerging *Homo sapiens* groveled in awe of his predecessors and awaited his own moment to assume the center of Earth's transient stage.

Because of my interest in the question of prehistoric civilizations, I prompted Starr Farish to ask the Source to speak in regard to the ancient myth of Lemuria. The sitting took place on June 29, 1972. Here is an edited transcript of that session.

Was there a lost nation that we call Lemuria?

Yes, there was a civilization that has been labeled Lemuria. The nation itself, or rather its land mass, was connected with other land masses with water on either side. This land mass extended from the corner of what is now the United States. It extended to, and included, what is now called the Hawaiian Islands.

The Hawaiian Islands were the southernmost boundary?

The land mass extended several hundred miles beyond the Hawaiian Islands, but they were included in the land mass, as such.

Was Orcas Island, where we live, a part of Lemuria?

Yes, the chain known as the San Juan Islands were a part of Lemuria, as well as Vancouver Island. They were all joined and formed a part of that great land mass.

Did it extend as far north as Alaska?

No.

Was any part of the United States or Canada a part of Lemuria?

The land masses at that time were quite different from the land masses today. Many small land masses have unified to become a joint land mass, thus forming North and South America. South America was once a part of the land mass you now call Africa.

Can this civilization be compared to that of Atlantis?

They were basically one and the same.

Did they co-exist?

There was a period when they did, but Lemuria is much older than Atlantis. These people whom you choose to call

118

Lemurian were very advanced. Many things, such as levitation and telepathy, were quite common.

Did some of the Lemurians then reincarnate in the Atlantean civilization?

Yes, and there was communication between the two civilizations, intelligent communication, although there were no wires strung.

What happened to Lemuria?

It sank due to a great cataclysm. Some parts of the continent remain, but much of it was segmented and engulfed by the waters. There will come a day—it is not far away—when evidence will be found to substantiate the existence of Lemuria.

Louis once told me of a land mass rising off the coast here. That would be a part of this ancient civilization, I assume. Would this correspond to the cataclysms which we all know and expect to happen in California within the next few years?

To a degree. The cataclysm that you expect in California will touch many areas, not only that state.

How was the Lemurian civilization different from that of the United States in its present stage of development?

There was a different rhythm, a different pattern. Lemuria did not have the monetary system as its guiding light. Lemurian culture was, in essence, communal. Their deep religious convictions and philosophies permeated all things in which they involved themselves.

Were people of Louis' abilities common?

Very common. He would have felt quite at home. The person who did not use these abilities was the one who was considered different or out of place.

Did they have physical vehicles for travel—airplanes, cars, trains, boats—or were such conveyances unnecessary?

They had such vehicles, yes. There were submarines and wingless airplanes. Their aircraft worked with a beam, not on the aerodynamic principles used today. They used magnetism.

Somewhat akin to the energy source that UFO's are thought to employ?

119

There is a similarity, yes. The UFO's also work on the gravitational theory.

What political structure governed the land?

The political structure, as we said, was communal. There were no heads of government, such as you see in the governmental patterns which emphasize kings or presidents. Twelve people sat on the Council, and it was they who made the decisions.

What colors were the skin and complexions of the nation's inhabitants?

They were fair, very fair. They were a tall people. The male usually stood around seven feet in height; the female, around six feet. They had the same basic bone structure as you have today.

Was there a system of marriage?

Not as you know it. There were people who were paired, but they did not have a piece of paper to prove it.

In what type of buildings did they house themselves?

Most of the buildings were made of stone. These were communal-type dwellings. A number of families would live in one dwelling, taking common meals together. Few buildings were over two or three stories in height. There was a love that permeated the atmosphere, the vibration. They respected themselves, and they respected each other.

The Lemurians had schools, but again, not like the schools with which you are familiar. The teachings were basically given by the parents of the children on an every-day, rather than school-day, basis.

What religious orthodoxies did the nation support?

There were temples, but no creeds or dogmas as you know them. Their religious philosophy was of brotherhood, one God, love. War, as you know it, was not known. There were differences of opinion, but these were settled around a table, not a battlefield. Theirs was a philosophy of love that one lived, not merely spoke.

According to our calendar, what dates or time period could we give to the existence of Lemuria? When was its Golden Age or its height of development? Edgar Cayce fixed Atlantis from about 150,000 B.C. to about 20,000 B.C., I believe.

Those dates are somewhat askew. Lemuria reached its decline about 150,000 years before the birth of the Christ.

Did any Lemurians survive the cataclysm?

Yes, there were survivors, who carried segments of their culture to other continents.

Lemuria was not the proper name for this nation, was it?

No, they called it Tadawnis. They were the people of Tadawnis.

Why was Tadawnis destroyed?

Why are people born? Why do people die? Why does the sun rise, and why does it set? It is all part of an evolutionary pattern that has been going on for aeons and will continue. It is the pattern of progression. It may not always appear to be progression, but it is, nevertheless. It was time for Tadawnis to end its chapter and for another to begin.

It would seem that we are preparing to enter another period of transition.

It is so. Many people know this. The cultural pattern of which you are a part is rapidly changing, restructuring. Within a hundred years, it will be difficult to recognize what is now from that which will be. This is part of change and growth. This is part of progress.

21

The Man Jesus

Editor's note: Of the man Jesus it has been written: "He was born in an obscure village. He worked in a carpenter shop until he was thirty. He then became an itinerant preacher. He never held office. He never had a family or owned a house. He didn't go to college. He had no credentials but himself. He was only thirty-three when the public turned against him. His friends ran away. He was turned over to his enemies and went through the mockery of a trial. He was nailed to a cross between two thieves. While he was dying, his executioners gambled for his clothing, the only property he had on earth. He was laid in a borrowed grave. Nineteen centuries have come and gone, and today he is the central figure of the human race. All the armies that ever marched, all the navies that ever sailed, all the parliaments that ever sat, and all the kings that ever reigned, have not affected the life of man on this earth as much as that one solitary life."

In this time of social chaos, crises, and depressions, millions of men and women are sensing an impending change, a period of transition, a time of spiritual rebirth. In such an emotional climate, it is not surprising that the Source should be questioned for details about the life of the single spiritual leader who has had the greatest effect upon the psyches of Western man.

The Source: Jesus was born on the outskirts of Bethlehem in a cave that had been dug on a hillside for the purpose of stabling cattle and other animals. He was born at midnight, a time which has much significance. Midnight is the time of highest vibrational frequency during the course of a day. Midnight represents a time of melding, of unifying, of harmonizing.

When Jesus was born, his birth was felt by many people. The birth was felt by the plant and animal life about, as well. The birds flocked to the grotto where he was born. There was a great vibrational feeling about the grotto.

When was Jesus born?

It does not really matter when Jesus was born, but the month was May.

Seven persons were present at the birth, with the child Jesus making the eighth. There were the innkeeper with his daughter, a midwife with husband and daughter, Mary and Joseph. Later they were joined by four wise men, two from the court of Herod. Altogether, there were twelve persons present at the birth. Jesus was a very beautiful baby, a very alert, very aware baby, but his birth was like that of any other birth.

Mary was a very beautiful young woman who had just turned sixteen. Joseph was thirty-eight. A big man, a strong man, a very manly man. He had been married prior to his union with Mary. Mary was very intuitive, very aware of the physical world, and yet, very aware of the unmanifested world.

Was Joseph the physical father of Jesus?

Oh, yes. He was especially chosen because of his strength and prowess. His semen was very fertile. There had to be the proper ingredients present to produce this child.

At the time of the birth of Jesus, King Herod knew that

something was going on in his realm. He had heard rumors about a special person being born. His wise men, his astrologers, and his court of psychic counselors had told him about this event that was forthcoming. Occasionally, during the enrollment of the people for tax purposes, King Herod would send out spies dressed as peasants to ask questions of the people about the special birth; and because he was rather intuitive, he would interpret these items of information as threats to his own well-being. He was becoming frightened. People seemed to be sensing a new awareness arriving, and Herod was afraid that one day his subjects would march into his court and place this special person, this true king, upon his throne. It was because of his own insecurity that Herod issued the proclamation that all the male children under the age of two should be killed. That is when Mary and Joseph took the child Jesus to Egypt.

They stayed with friends in a small village until Jesus was seven. Joseph supported them as a craftsman. He was an excellent carpenter and a very intelligent man, as well.

Did Joseph ever marry Mary, or did they just live together and come to be accepted as man and wife?

Their marriage was not as you know marriage. Joseph had children before he married Mary, and they had two sons and a daughter born of their union after Jesus.

Did Jesus know of his mission as a child?

Unlike other avatars, Jesus knew of his mission from the time of his birth. But, of course, his physical vehicle had to catch up with his intuitive capacity. You must remember that a spiritual giant had been born into a tiny body. The body had to have time to stretch and grow, physically and psychologically.

Then when he was grown, he had full awareness?

Yes, Jesus had had many incarnations, but they were not the glamorous ones that have sometimes been indicated.

When did his schooling begin?

First of all, Jesus did not need to be schooled. All that he needed for his earth experience had been built into him—programmed, computerized, whatever you want to call it. But there were those who were sent to him—and we are speaking of earthly people—who aided in his education.

All Jesus' parents or teachers had to do was to expose him to various matters and instantly there was a recall, a recognition—it was all there. But as we said before, this was a very gradual process; because, remember, he was in a human body. People have always tended to dehumanize Jesus, but he was a human being.

Did Jesus ever have a sexual relationship?

Yes.

Was this for a very specific reason, or just because he wanted to?

It was for a specific reason, but it was a very, very minor part of his life. He was not a sexual being.

And Jesus was in this village until he was seven years of age, simply gaining experience and growing?

Actually, he was also teaching from the age of seven on.

Did Jesus have a diet different from that of other people?

Basically, Jesus and his family ate very simple foods. The dietary pattern was very different then from what is known today. There was no breakfast, lunch, and dinner. People ate a little food whenever they felt hungry. Elaborate meals came only at festive occasions. Today, man has a regimen of eating. For Jesus, a meal might have been a handful of dates or some milk—perhaps some milk and some bread.

What did Jesus look like, physically, as an adult?

He was not heavy-set, but he was a good-sized man like his father. He was several inches taller than the average man of his day. He was a very handsome man with reddish-blond hair. His eyes would change in color from blue to hazel. He had large eyes with very long eyelashes. He had great magnetism, great charisma.

Everybody loved this man, even if they did not know why. They loved him even as a child; people just couldn't do enough for him. People loved to touch him and do things for him.

What was the reason for the apparent color change of his eyes?

The color of his eyes changed depending on what was taking place within his totality at the time. When he became very pensive, very close to the Father, he would gaze upward and his eyes would become very blue. When he was working with the people and talking to them, his eyes would become a very warm brown. There are many people who have this change in eye pigmentation today. There is nothing supernatural about it.

Jesus was not a supernatural being. He was a human being with tremendous insight and awareness. He admonished people over and over not to worship him, but that for which he stood.

Was this the last of Jesus' incarnations?

Yes. He had had many incarnations, but this was his final one.

Was the general pattern of his life to travel from village to village as a teacher?

Yes. At first he came into contact only with the very wise ones. As he grew older, he exposed more of his instructions to the unknowing ones. You see, someone who is wise can accept truth in many forms, even from a child; but the general populace cannot. Jesus did not really work with the masses until he had reached physical maturity.

All of his lifetime, Jesus did much of what is called bilocation, being in more than one place at a time. That is why the man Jesus had been reported to have been in so many lands, when, actually, in the physical body, he never traveled more than a few miles from the place of his birth.

He traveled in an astral, a nonphysical form?

Those who saw him, saw a solid form. He went wherever there was wisdom, so that he might share. Teaching can be a very sterile thing. Teaching is an intellectual process, whereas sharing is done from the heart and affords the greatest learning tool that there is.

Jesus went to share. He said so often, "Let your light shine out before them." You see, you can share with a person without saying a word. You can share your vibration, your aura, with him.

What did Jesus mean when, upon the cross, he cried: "Father, why hast thou forsaken me?"

127

He did not say that. These are the words that have been passed down. What he actually said was, "Father, I am ready."

Jesus' teachings have been very much misunderstood, and much perversion of his words has taken place down through the centuries. To speak of the Father forsaking one would be the words of one with little consciousness, not the words of one with the Christ Consciousness.

If the words of Jesus and other great avatars have been misinterpreted by those who have passed them down to our age, what can we believe of what we read?

You must go within. Within each man is the truth, within each man burns the candle of the light of truth. Within each man there is a knowing. Ultimately, all who seek truth must go within and *know.*

Basically, Jesus taught a very simple doctrine of love. He may have been the greatest avatar of all, for he over-intellectualized the least. His was the philosophy of simplicity. Regrettably, his teachings have been added to like that of a stone rolling slowly down a hillside gathering moss, until the present-day concept of Jesus' philosophy has become verbose, redundant, and over-intellectualized until its essence has been all but killed.

22

*Q*uestion and Answer
Session with the Source

Editor's note: The following questions and answers have been
selected from numerous readings given over a period of about
five years.

*How can I best help my children to express their higher
selves?*
By teaching them who they are and what they are; by
reminding them that they are bodies filled with God, Spirit,
perfection. Don't try to control their lives. Do try to give them
freedom.

Will the lost continent of Atlantis arise?
In time, in time. It is happening now. But it will not fully
rise until various cataclysms have taken place in the United
States and other countries. Some land masses must sink so that
they may rise.

*Jeane Dixon and others refer to an anti-Christ who has
already been born. Can you explain this, please?*

The anti-Christ is within each person; it is not a human being. The anti-Christ is going on in all the war, hate, greed, and envy which you see about you. This is your anti-Christ.

The Christ spirit is a spiraling, almost fountain-like motion. The anti-Christ movement is more static.

The Christ spirit flows and builds. The anti-Christ stagnates and destroys.

There will be no man, no two-legged man, who will be called the anti-Christ.

How does one know his purpose in life?
If one will ask, he will know and he will be led. It has been stated many times, "Ask and ye shall receive." But too many people, when asking their true purpose in life, say, "Oh, no, that is not me," when they are shown. They do not realize that serving the Father is not always something glamorous and spectacular.

What happens to the spirit between incarnations?
That depends upon the spirit. Usually it goes to a place of learning.

Is it all right to spread the word about metaphysical teachings?
You are not to proselyte. Do not force these concepts upon people. If someone should ask a question of you, you then have a duty to give him that question's answer. You must give information only to those who are ready, and they will signal their presence by asking questions. You feed only the hungry, for only they have appetites.

Does astrology work? Is it a good way in which to chart your life?
Astrology forms a pattern. One can follow this pattern; one can learn from it; or one can be very fanciful with it and use it for marvelous daydreams. Astrology can be a meaningful tool or a childish plaything, depending upon the individual practitioner.

130

Do I have a spirit guarding me?
Yes and no. God is spirit, but you do not have a spirit guide guarding you, as such. But the God within, which is spirit, guards you, depending upon your thinking.

Remember, as you go along in life, it is your thought processes which determines what happens to you. If you think horrible things are going to happen to you, we assure you that they will happen. If you look for the beautiful things, the constructive things—at the same time realizing that you came into this life to give and not to take—yours will truly be a glorious life.

No one needs to guard you. It is not necessary.

What is the main purpose in life and how should I go about achieving it?
Everyone's main purpose—and this goes for the whole of mankind—is to expand the consciousness, the spiritual awareness, the One-ness with God.

If God is merciful, why is there so much misery and hurt in the world?
One must not look upon God as being merciful or unmerciful, for to do so places God into the category of man. It would be like saying that God feels pain or God has a headache and, consequently, he must take an aspirin.

Terms such as mercy or merciful put God on a human level. For centuries man has tried to reduce God to his own dimensions. We cannot equate God on these terms.

If there is injustice, if there is strife, it is caused by man, not God. It is man's misuse of the Divine Principle and Laws that bring these things about.

If hard times are coming, how can we best prepare for them?
By simplifying your life and knowing how to do without. By being self-sufficient, by being able to raise your own foods, to make your own clothes. The secret is to simplify your life and to be happy with what you have.

Take your family into the country and remain as a unit, working together, talking together, meditating together. It is not by accident that you came together this lifetime. It is not by accident that there is a tremendous love vibration about you. Your love vibration, together with your being together, will protect you from the negative influences of the difficult times ahead.

I tend to over-intellectualize, and this leads to confusion.
When you intellectualize, you dissect. If you have a lovely little dog and you want to understand that dog, do you take a knife and cut it apart? You would find out all about your dog, but you would have killed it. This is what you do when you over-intellectualize. You tear things apart into many pieces, leaving yourself no whole when you are finished.

You need to be cognizant of things, aware of things, but aware on an intuitive level, not an intellectual level. Knowing and knowing about are two different things. When you intellectualize, you know about. When you go within, you know.

Why was Jesus crucified?
Every man is crucified. Jesus suffered a physical crucifixion, but every man has his own time of crucifixion. It is this crucifixion that gives him the strength to go forward, to go onward, to release, and to go beyond that thin wall. Had not this man been crucified, his life would not have had the meaning that it has for the millions today. It was necessary that this act of total giving be performed so that each man could comprehend, in his own way, that he, too, must give.

How might one best spread the message of unity in Awareness to others without appearing strange or kookie in their eyes? How might we best communicate with others and help them to raise their Awareness?
By being a shining example. Examples are the best teachers. One need do nothing more than become an example.

Is it possible on this physical plane, in our physical lives, to be completely balanced within oneself without a mate?

132

It is very helpful to have a mate. Without a mate the job is difficult, but it can be done. In some instances, people are not prepared for a mate: Their Karmic pattern is so structured that they must do it on their own. This is not the easy route, but at times it must be done.

You see, when one has a mate, there is a blending and a molding and a lifting, which adds much joy to one's life. There are those, however, who must travel another path. It is more difficult, but they can both arrive at the same destination—and that destination is balance.

How may I be strengthened in order that I may be of service to others?

First, you must develop your own awareness, your own self, your own reality. You must gain spiritual strength and spiritual confidence. You need to impregnate your totality until the time comes when you know that you are ready to go forward and to serve. You must serve self first, and after you have saturated self, you can go forward. Now you have something to give. You have inner strength; you have inner knowledge. You can lift others.

Study, expose yourself to the writings of those who are truly wise. Enter a program of meditation, a time of silence, a time of One-ness. Be that which you believe, become a shining example, and you will be prepared to serve mankind.

Are there such things as spirits? If so, what are they and where are they?

When man leaves the dwelling that he calls a body, there are times when that energy which dwelt within the body is drawn back to the earth plane. These energies are referred to as spirits. Yes, they do exist, but many people place too much emphasis on these spirits and do not perceive the total picture.

Do some spirits have difficulty transcending?

There are some spirits that do not know that they are no longer in the body on the earth plane; consequently, they linger.

133

Do they then become what some people refer to as ghosts?
Yes, but in time they will reach a fuller consciousness and transcend to other planes of consciousness.

Does God stand waiting to punish every wrong deed?
No. This is a tragic misconception that people have. There is no angry God waiting to punish us. There is no such thing as sin; there is no such thing as wrong or right, in essence. We all come to this life to give and to live abundantly, in peace, harmony, and joy.

The old religions taught that there was a vindictive God, waiting to strike out when one trespassed the line of righteousness; but this is not so.

One should try to live a constructive life; one should try to give to life each day. The pattern that should be projected is one of love, not constant fear. As we get to know love, as we become love, all those things that we call problems will turn to smoke and pass very rapidly.

Why do obstacles arise to block so many of my efforts?
For some reason, you seem to think that you are inferior. You seem to think that you have less ability, less awareness, less personality than others. And even now I hear you silently intoning excuses to yourself.

You have a great amount of intelligence to share with others; and beyond that, you have a tremendous soul force to share.

You have love within you that does not come out. You need to relax and let go and permit the spiritual awareness within yourself to grow and to expand and to permeate the totality.

Basically, you are very aware. But it is as if you will not allow your awareness to become a part of your total pattern.

Begin to walk tall, to walk proud. Begin to realize who you are and what you are.

Are you not a part of God? And is not God perfect? Is not God expansive, all-knowing? Then, are not these qualities within you?

You must not deny that from which you come or that of which you are a part, because in so denying, you will shut off the source, you will short-circuit the cosmic universe.

Begin to know, not from an intellectual, but an intuitive level. You are indeed capable of fantastic things.

Up to this point you have expressed very little of what you really are. In the days ahead, remind yourself who you really are and what you really are, and your days will be filled with the sunshine that comes not from without, but from within.

At the conclusion of a reading on March 8, 1970, the Source uttered an admonition that might profit each sincere seeker:

The answer to any problem is to have an expansive nature, to become so filled with Love that nothing can challenge you. This is the best thing that we can tell you: Be Love. Fill yourself with Love. Give the world Love in its true sense of serving, of giving. Be not concerned with what you get out of life. Remember, the man who puts the most wood into the fire gets back the warmest blaze. Feed life all the Love that you can, and that Love will come back to you manyfold.

23

---

*R*emedies and
Recipes for Health

Editor's note: The following remedies and recipes for health were distilled from dozens of readings which cover approximately a five-year period. These remedies were, in most instances, given by the Source to be used by specific individuals. Just as every prescription issued by a medical doctor will not prove beneficial to every patient, so it may be that certain of these remedies and recipes may be more effective for some people than for others. They are included in this text for the reader's information, and they are not intended to supplant sound medical practice or recognized programs of health care.

On canning: Most canned foods are worthless and not to be used.

Fifty percent of the foods you eat should be raw. When you do cook foods, try to cook without boiling—steaming is recommended.

One exception is tomato juice; canned tomato juice appears in several recipes. Canned milk has some value, but the enzymes are lost in the processing.

Foods should be grown in a balanced soil. A humus or compost is recommended as follows: charcoal, sulfur, iron, silicon. The iron can come from grass clippings; sawdust and steer manure are also recommended. Sand will provide the silicon.

Iron, a stabilizer, and copper, an energizer, are both very important to the body. Dark-green vegetables are a source of iron. Copper can be found in apricots, honey, and sunflower seeds.

Potassium aids the intuitive powers.

Too much calcium can cause warts; this is associated with a poor skin.

Pectin is beneficial to the stomach, intestines, and colon. The liquid form is easier to use, but the powdered form is just as good. A juice diet, coupled with three bottles (four- or six-ounce size) of liquid pectin per day is recommended for gastrointestinal upsets.

Schizophrenia is an unbalance of polarities, an imbalance of the whole structure.

Depression is caused by past experiences triggered off by chemical imbalances in the body. Frequently, this is due to lack of iron. Iron tablets, blackstrap molasses, or deep-green salads may help this.

Man will go back to some of the natural approaches. He will learn that his food, his thoughts, his religion, or his philosophy is his medicine—not something in a little bottle with a label on it. In the year 2000 there will be some rather remarkable forward steps in healing. What we know today as "cancer" will not exist, nor will many of the so-called problems of today.

REMEDIES

Warts
Dab vinegar on the warts every day for a month, or tape a vitamin C tablet on each wart every day for thirty days. When the warts are gone, rub the area with olive oil to prevent them from coming back.

Circulation problems in extremities
Soak in hot water.

Rub with hot oil.
Heat with heating pad or hot-water bottle.

Psoriasis

Vitamins E and A. Take hot baths in baking soda and water: ½
cup of soda to a tub of water. Air-baths and sun-baths are also
recommended.

Laxative

1 cup cooked prunes	1 cup honey
1 cup liquid pectin	1 cup charcoal, powdered
1 cup bran	1 scant teaspoon croton oil

(1 cup olive or pure wheat-germ oil in addition is optional)
Mix the ingredients.
Dosage: One tablespoonful of the mixture.

Diarrhea

Pectin and blackberry juice combined in equal amounts will aid in
overcoming diarrhea. It is preferable to use fresh or frozen berries
and juice them in a blender. Use no other foods at the time. Take
the mixture in half-cup amounts every three hours.

Vomiting

Pectin and coconut milk in equal proportions will help control
vomiting.

Colitis and other stomach disorders

Liquid pectin, generally in four- to six-ounce doses, three times
daily.

Digestive problems

Use the skins of fruits: pear, apple, pineapple, etc., but *not* bananas.
Simmer two or three minutes in water, cool and strain. Drink the
same day. Acidophilus culture will also help digestive problems.

Hemorrhoids

1 pound yellow petroleum jelly
1 ounce pure iodine (not the tincture)
Mix and warm in the sun or in a pan of warm water to melt
the petroleum jelly and permit the iodine to dissolve in it.
Cool and use as a rectal salve one week to ten days.

Anemia or "Tired Blood"

1 cup raw honey, preferably tupelo or buckwheat honey	1 cup almond meal
	6 raw eggs

139

1 cup blackstrap molasses
Place in a blender and mix. Take three tablespoonfuls per day.
preferably morning, noon, and night. One tablespoon of this mixture can also be dissolved in one cup warm raw milk to make a
drink. Continue for ten days or more.

Potassium broth
Vegetable peelings: carrot, potato, etc., add water and boil two to
three minutes. Let stand and cool; pour liquid through muslin cloth.
Store in a covered jar; drink the same day. Provides a good source
of supplementary potassium.

Kidney condition
For kidney stones or inflamed kidneys:
1 cup pure grape juice
1 teaspoon cream of tartar.
Mix. Take one or two ounces three times a day. This is also good
for bed-wetting problems in children, especially if one teaspoon raw
honey is added to the mixture.

Insomnia
1 cups milk (any kind: skim, powdered, whole), warmed to body
temperature
1 small head of lettuce, quartered
Blend these together in a blender and drink immediately.

Stress, especially due to change
Vitamin B in large quantities
Iron and iron-rich foods
Licorice
Rest

Asthma
One ounce each: wintergreen oil
                 oil of peppermint
                 oil of cloves
                 orange oil
                 linseed oil
Mix in one pint glycerine and use as a chest rub. This is especially
good for children at bedtime.

140

Nasal congestion or sore throat
1 pint pure spring water
1 tablespoon sea salt
Bring water to a boil, add salt; let cool.
Use as a gargle.
Use this diluted (half-and-half with more pure spring water) as an
eyewash; if used regularly this way, it will prevent cataracts.

Heart and respiratory conditions
Agitate pure spring water in a blender and drink immediately.

Cataracts (already formed)
1 quart pure spring water   5000 units vitamin C (Ascorbic acid)
1 tablespoon powdered alum   1 drop pure iodine.
Use as an eye rinse frequently. This mixture will also help shrink
tumorous conditions about the eyes.

Arthritis and rheumatism
For easing the pain of arthritis (also of strains and sprains), a
rubbing mixture is recommended as follows:
1 pint rubbing alcohol
25 aspirins, powdered
Mix. Add 4 ounces wintergreen oil.
Shake and apply locally.

Bruises, swellings, sunburn, sprains, etc.
1 pint rubbing alcohol
1 cup wintergreen oil
1 cup eucalyptus oil
Use as a general rubdown; also excellent for reducing a high fever.

Douche for female infections
2 cups water
1 cup hydrogen peroxide
3000 units vitamin C

Facepack for acne
1 pound white clay
1 cup oatmeal
1 cup dry powdered eggs
Mix with hydrogen peroxide to make a pack of a consistency to apply.

141

Facepack for wrinkles
1 cup raw honey   1 cup apricot oil
1 fresh raw egg   1 cup clay powder
1 cup water with 3 tablespoons Epsom salts dissolved in it
Mix carefully. Store in a tightly closed jar in the refrigerator. Apply
daily before retiring; leave on for about 15 minutes, then wash off
with warm water.

Hair rinse
Dissolve 1 ounce pure gelatine in 1 cup hot water. Cool. Add 7
drops of apricot oil.
Apply to hair after shampooing.

Headache
1 quart brewed Green tea
2 to 3 lemons, squeezed, and with the rind cut up.
Add the juice and rind to the tea while hot; let cool, strain, and
drink. Do not add sugar or honey.

Mononucleosis
This is caused by a virus linked to a chain or spectrum of viruses
of which the most deadly is the cancer virus; toward the other end
is the common cold. "Valley Fever" is also related to this. A high
vitamin C program (9000 units daily) is recommended for mono-
nucleosis, combined with some dairy product (milk or cream), and
rest.

Along with this should go a saturation program of therapeutic
vitamins, everything from A to G, plus minerals. A sparse diet of
fruit and vegetable juices should accompany this. Hot baths and
massage should be used to increase circulation.

Pinched sciatic nerve
3000 units of vitamin C daily (six 500 mg. tablets) for 30 days.
Remove all starches and sugars from the diet for 30 days (a rare
piece of bread is all right, but nothing more).
Use a poultice or pack as follows:
1 pound Epsom salts
2 pounds white clay powder
Dissolve Epsom salts in one quart boiling water; cool to tepid and
slowly add the clay powder. Make a pack of it and apply from the
buttock on down the leg. Leave on 30 minutes; it will harden. This
should be done once a day. To remove, use a hot bath with Epsom

142

salts dissolved in it. It is rather messy, and is more easily done in the bathroom.

Tranquilizer
1 cup lemon juice
2 heaping tablespoons brewer's yeast
2 tablespoons wheat germ
Mix. Add 1 quart or large can tomato juice.

Energizers
1 cup freshly squeezed orange juice (or frozen orange juice if necessary)   1 raw egg
1 tablespoon honey   1 tablespoon wheat germ oil
Optional: 2 to 3 almonds; 1 tablespoon sunflower seeds; dash lemon juice.
Blend.
   or
1 cup raisins   1 cup blackstrap molasses
1 cup honey   6 raw eggs
Blend or mix to form a paste.
Add 1 tablespoon of this paste to 1 cup tepid or warm milk, in blender or by hand.
This mixture is rich in iron.

VITAMINS

Vitamin A
This basically affects the outward covering of the human anatomy—the skin. Vitamin A is useful for burns, combined with a white clay and sterile (boiled or distilled) water poultice.

Vitamin B
A tranquilizer. Good for the nerves, the brain, the nerve endings, the cortexes. Any nerve deficiency will be aided by vitamin B.

Vitamin C
The cleanser of the body. It fights any type of infection that comes into the body. Sometimes massive doses are required. For a serious infection, it might be necessary to take 50,000 to 60,000 units daily.

Vitamin D
The "sunshine vitamin," it works basically on the skeletal frame of the body, the bones, the anatomy.

143

Vitamin E
Works basically on the muscular system.

SUGGESTIONS FOR A GOOD DIET

Breakfast
Fresh fruit or fresh juice: berries, pineapple, apples, etc.
2 eggs, poached or soft-boiled
1 piece of bread or a muffin (preferably a health-grain muffin)
Beverage: Coffee is good at breakfast, because it stimulates the bowels

Lunch
Vegetable salad with all sorts of fresh vegetables
Cheese or sunflower seeds in the salad for protein
Bit of dressing
    or
Hot bowl of vegetables
Fruit: orange or apple

Dinner
Steamed or baked vegetables
Whole-grain muffin

24

The True Meaning and Significance of Sex

The Source: Many human beings do not even know what sex is. In essence, it's a blending of polarities, a uniting. The aspect known as intercourse is primarily for the bringing forth of individuals into the world. Most people do not approach this as they should.

So you can have sex without having intercourse?

So many people have what they call "hang-ups" in the area of sex which produce all sorts of fears, guilts, anxieties, and frustrations.

What are their hang-ups built upon?

Parental and sociological do's and don'ts.

Misguidance?

Yes.

Not as far as intercourse is concerned, but as far as sex is concerned?

Yes. You see, there are two main divisions. If sex is the result of lust, then it takes on a negative connotation; but if it is truly a part of love, then it takes on a positive connotation.

So, theoretically, you could experience sex any time throughout the day?

Yes, exactly.

Theoretically, you can express sex with no one else around.

Yes, and you do not have to express it with the opposite sex. Which is quite shocking to many people.

Intercourse must be expressed with others, if it's to bring others into the world.

Exactly; but many people do not realize that the handshake, for example, is a sexual gesture.

Is there a blending of polarities in that?

Yes. The playing of tennis is a sexual thing if you take it in its broadest connotation. The spectrum of sex is much broader than most people realize. Sex is not limited to the bedroom.

What do you think about celibacy?

In some cases it may be a very good thing, if the individual finds that this is an aid to his growth pattern. But just as with vegetarianism and many other things, it depends upon the individual.

If one's polarities were completely balanced, then I would think he would be having a sexual experience or expressing a sexual side at all times. To have both polarities completely balanced, would require a very special person, wouldn't it?

Yes.

Might such an individual ascribe to celibacy because he would have no need outside of his own self?

Yes.

But most people need to meld with other people in order to attain balance?

This is correct. For some, sexual expressions, or physical or a bedroom expression, are not important; they can find their expression in other things.

How does sex relate to other creative energies?

Although you have the ability to channel the creative energy that your reproductive organs produce in any manner that you desire, it is most difficult to direct your creative energy for more than one activity at the same time and do justice to any. To be truly creative you must devote all your energies to one focal point. And then, after the culmination of the creative aspect, you should rest so that your body has the

146

opportunity to recharge the batteries, for you will have "run yourself down."

Consider the following: If you gave a person an I.Q. test directly following an orgasm, after the use of a great amount of creative energy, you would find that the results would be a test score much less than if the "batteries" were completely charged—probably 23 to 30 points less. You should never attempt to focus your creative energies on more than one thing at one time, and you should never attempt to use your creative energy directly following a great exertion of creative energy until you are recharged.

The recharging period depends upon many factors and the time necessary for recharging can be different for each individual. It can depend upon your health, your state of mind, and so on. Actually, you begin recharging immediately after the use of any creative energy. The tired feeling after an orgasm (physical, mental, or spiritual) is the body's way of telling you to relax and let the current start flowing again; to permit the physical body to relax so that the normal body energy can be used to recharge the batteries instead of being used for exertive bodily functions. If you have an orgasm and immediately pursue an activity such as dancing, it would be very difficult on the body, for you would be asking it to perform two energy tasks at once.

What is the real purpose behind marriage?

Some people get married because their parents did, or because their friends are, or because they are told that it is the thing to do. Actually, probably one person in twenty-five knows the purpose of marriage.

Physical sex also plays a great part in the marriage concept, and many persons are married for that reason alone. The very young especially do this, for their sex drive (the amount of creative energy produced) is more pronounced than in those who are older. Also, they do not know how to direct this abundance of energy. Marriage, however, is not for the purpose of having intercourse night after night. Intercourse is for the purpose of bearing offspring. Marriage is for the purpose of sexual relations. Real marriage is a total sexual involvement, a

147

process of melding and uniting with another person for the benefit of both. It may sometimes be in the form of intercourse, but it is a sexual involvement at all times.

What makes a successful marriage, then?

Wisdom is the key to a successful marriage. An individual must be wise enough to pick that person for his or her mate who best complements his or her own particular vibrational pattern. In other words, choose that person whose magnetic or electrical forces flow best with yours. This is the masculine and feminine concept; this is a balancing of polarities.

The main purpose of marriage is to combine two energies that complement one another for the sexual act, the *real* sexual act. Physical intercourse is a secondary consideration. If you marry someone who absolutely complements your polarity, you will have a *perfect* marriage—a marriage with the universe. This is the *ultimate,* and you will meld and blend with the Cosmos.

Intercourse, sex, and marriage are not inseparable?

It is obvious that you need not have physical intercourse to partake in *real* sex, and you do not have to be married to have a marriage. You need only mingle. Some doctors, for example, blend better with their nurses than they do with their own marriage partners. This may be a reason for their success, since they may be melding with this associate and responding to a sexual mingling. They are married, then, and perhaps they do not even know it.

Since we are all striving to balance ourselves, and this may be difficult to accomplish by ourselves alone, another person may lend his vibrational force field to complement and to balance our own.

What should a couple expect of a marriage?

Marriage is a divine sacrament. It is the unifying of two souls for a common goal. It should be one of the most beautiful experiences for two human beings. Many people say that they are going into marriage on a fifty-fifty basis; but one must give his all to marriage if he hopes to receive the full value from it. Marriage is one of the glorious sacraments. Hold it precious, hold it as holy.

If marriage is holy, is it ever right to end one?

Yes, there are times when two people are to spend a short period of time together. We might have a marriage of one day, of one month, of one year, or one lifetime. But end it in love, not in hate.

Why do some seek relations with the same sex?

Since sex is a co-mingling of forces, perhaps this helps explain why those who are known as bi-sexuals or homosexuals find comfort in expressing themselves as they do. Many feminine males and many masculine females find it difficult to blend their polarities with someone of the opposite sex. They are unable to meld with them, so they resort to a melding with someone of the same sex. Basically, they balance their polarity, not with someone of the opposite sex as with the majority of society, but with someone of the same sex.

Does it matter with whom you have sexual relations, then?

One should have great caution regarding with whom he or she has a physical sexual relationship. This marriage or co-mingling of force fields has a long-term effect and can influence the remainder of your life.

For example, if you had copulation with a person some years ago and that person had a negative personality, that person can still drain on your being now, no matter what the distance, no matter how long the elapsed time. That one-time vibrational bond is an all-time tie. All sexual relationships, on any level, connote greater influences than may appear on the surface.

25

The Awareness of the American Indian

Louis: I have an aunt and uncle who had a trading post on the Navajo reservation. As a child I used to visit them, and I was quite accepted by the Indians. They seemed aware that I was psychic.

Later, as a young man, I became quite well-acquainted with the Hopis, and I went through a brotherhood ceremony. I think I am still considered to be something akin to a medicine man, or something of that caliber, by the Hopi.

The thing that has always fascinated me about the American Indians is their philosophy of One-ness. They believe that the rocks, the plants, everything is sacred and all part of a whole, a single grand design. And they live their lives in accordance with that philosophy.

I remember Aunt Mabel and Uncle Jim telling of the time that the United States government wanted to teach the Navajos how to raise corn. The Indians have been raising corn for thousands of years, even though it is not that tall Iowa kind of corn. They go about raising their corn in a very religious way. They plant the kernels, chant over them, and conduct a ceremony of blessing.

The government came up and took a plot of land right next to where the Indians had their fields. They were going to show them how to grow corn. They brought their machines, and they plowed the land and fertilized it. They brought certain super hybrid varieties of corn, and they put two kernels into the soil next to where the Navajos had planted their corn.

Come harvest time, the Indians' corn was twice as high as the government's corn, and the government agriculturalists just couldn't understand why. The Navajos, however, understood the law of vibration.

Recent experiments with plants have demonstrated that plants do have consciousness and that they do respond to vibrations. I think if I were a seed or a plant, I would respond much better to a very tender, loving placement in the soil than I would to being placed there by a very cold piece of machinery.

My mother has very vivid recall of a lifetime as a Pueblo Indian. We have gone to this area where the Pueblos lived, and she has showed us the trails that she once walked and the place where she used to dwell.

I have no recollection of ever having been involved with the American Indian in any way during my past lifetimes. I seem to have been most often in the Orient. I think if there is a vibrational tie-up between myself and the American Indians, it is because the Indians may be connected with a part of the ancient Oriental culture.

I am very taken with the Indian's love of simplicity and his honoring of truthfulness. He has a sensitivity toward all life that we of European ancestry seem to have put aside many, many years ago. I think man needs to return to this feeling, this sensing, this awareness of both the exterior and the interior worlds. The Indian recognizes the intuitive point of view, as well as the intellectual. The white man is just now coming to recognize the existence of this inner awareness.

Do I have any predictions for the American Indian? Well, I think right now that there are many hostility patterns which are coming forth, and I think that some of them are really defeating Indian goals, rather than helping them.

But I feel that there is a coming-back for the Indian, a return to tradition, a return to pride, a return to a sensitivity that flourished better before the white man bulldozed down the trees and dammed up the streams to make electricity.

I feel that the American Indian will experience a return of the spirit that was once felt all over this land. There will be a revival of pride in what it means to be an Indian.

Both the white and the red brothers and sisters will understand the part they play in one another's lives. They will see that nothing happens by accident.

The white man will begin to take the Indian seriously; he will recognize his red brother's art, his music.

The white man will acknowledge the red man as a person with depth. The image of the savage, the pagan, will disappear and leave in its place the picture of a people with nobility and worth.

26

*P*reparing for the
New Age

Question: I study and read a lot, and I am well aware of the terrible times ahead. Can you see an approximate time and year when the time of transition will be completed?
The Source: In the year 2000, we shall enter into a time of completion, but until that time, there will still be inadequacies in the functioning of man.

I want to know if there will be much physical destruction during the time of transition?

Yes, the entire globe will change and vary. There will be water where there is none today. There will be mountains where there are none today. Mountains will rise and mountains will fall. New oceans will be formed. There will be a geological reformation.

For most who do not understand the time of transition, it will be a terribly upsetting time, because this period represents change. Man sometimes becomes very upset when he learns of forthcoming change. He seems to think that change is a negative thing, when in essence, man could not exist if it were not for change.

Because so many men and women are concerned about the

coming New Age which will be heralded by oft-predicted cata-clysms and earth changes, it was decided by the group on Orcas Island to hold a session on October 31, 1973, along the theme "Preparing for the New Age."

What is meant by "new" and what is meant by "age"? In actuality, there is no such thing as "New Age" or "Old Age." This "age" that is referred to by so many represents a time period that has already begun. It represents a time period marked with many changes—social, economic, geographical, and geological. It is most difficult for most human beings to accept change, and most who do accept it do so in a somewhat apathetic, negative way.

We must take into consideration that change is growth and growth is change. Old patterns are cast aside and new ones come forward. The days ahead will require one prime preparation and that is of attitude—an attitude of a positive, constructive nature; an attitude that is balanced and allows for flexibility. Those who are rigid will break psychologically and, in some cases, physically; but those with a positive attitude will be able to accept this time of restructuring. It is really a most exciting time, a time of tremendous vibrational patterns.

When do you feel the New Age will begin?

It actually began about the year of 1962.

Was there a representation in the heavens at that time?

Yes, and many were aware of this. Some read it as the world coming to an end, rather than as a new beginning. The political restructuring that you see going on today is all part of this large pattern.

Is the teenager of today more prepared for the New Age than the teenager of, say, twenty years ago would have been? What is the quality that makes today's teenagers seem more flexible?

Young people are generally influenced by certain environmental and hereditary patterns. Today we find young people who reject, rather than accept, many of the old patterns and hypocrasies. They are striving for new approaches to life.

There is an incarnation pattern that has been coming about for some years now, since the 1960's and a bit before. This pattern has given birth to some very inquiring young people who are looking for answers outside the traditional forms of knowledge. In so doing, they have set up a pattern which touches many people. It is good; it is constructive.

Today's youth are interested in expanding their horizons. They are not concerned with *a* place and *an* idea; they are concerned with places and ideas. They are helping to bring about the necessary changes.

Has the vibrational pattern of the Earth been accelerated as it enters this New Age? Or is it really the same vibrational level with different happenings occurring within its confines?

It is basically the same vibration, but there is a new rhythm, a new order being introduced.

As we enter this period and find some people working toward greater flexibility and others incarnating with greater flexibility, there seems to be an equal surge in the direction of conservatism, rigidity, and tension—especially in the realm of religion and people's viewpoint toward the intangible dimensions.

But these people are only a small percentage compared to those who are becoming more flexible. They are a minority. For some, it is necessary to enter a period of inflexibility. This is also a preparation.

Right now so many people are returning to essentials. Many are turning their backs on a world of gadgetry and are asking themselves what man really needs to live, to grow, to express. They are asking what foods man really needs for nutrition.

One must constantly remember that these changes are, in essence, constructive moves, constructive patterns, which will enable man to enter a period of refining, polishing, and distilling. Man is moving toward this thing called Brotherhood, this thing called Peace. These ideals will become reality.

When will the great earth changes begin?

If you want timing on this, you could say within the next five years.

What is the reason for this?

It is not reason that is behind it. It is a part of change, a restructuring, a part of the new cycle.

The new rhythm?

The new rhythm, the new movement. Much of what you had in the past was a time of stagnation. All aspects of life were reaching a point of stagnation. A stagnant pool must be drained and filled with new, clean water. This is what will be taking place. It is not a negative thing. It is not a thing to be afraid of.

The time of preparation is upon you. You must prepare mentally with your thought processes, and you must prepare physically. Both elements are necessary, for they are part of the whole One.

Evolution is nothing but change, growth, restructuring. The stuff you call matter is God in manifestation. Everything is alive, vibrating, changing in structure. When things cease to move, they reach the condition known as death, which is merely a transition, a walking from one room to another. It is brief, but it is necessary in the process of change.

Some people come upon this earth and bring forth some of these strange, so-called "new" ideas and concepts. They are the forerunners, the prologue-makers. They come to prepare those who are ready at that time. Eventually, the masses become aware of the message. It was the same with Jesus and all the great ones who came. The world into which they came was not prepared for what they had to give, but as time passes, consciousness changes; and that which they delivered to the earth takes on a different meaning to those of new understanding.

How does one prepare for the New Age? One gets his spiritual house in order, then as he walks down the road of life, he is prepared. He is ready for that which is around the next corner. It is those people who do not have their spiritual houses in order who will be befuddled and frightened about the changes which lie ahead.

Index

167